A STUDY OF HOME ™
~ special places

Editor	Bruce Arant
Plans Editor	Tina Leyden
Graphic Designers	Yen Gutowski
	Heather Guthrie
	Jeff Dedlow
Rendering Colorization	Beth Davis
	Alva Louden
Rendering Illustrators	Silvia Boyd
	Shawn Doherty
	George McDonald, dec.
	Gerald Metzger
Technical Adviser	Rob Phillips
Writer	Joyce Brown
Circulation Manager	Priscilla Ivey
Co-Publishers	Dennis Brozak
	Linda Reimer

A STUDY OF HOME ™
~ special places

IS PUBLISHED BY:
Design Basics Publications
11112 John Galt Blvd., Omaha, NE 68137
web – www.designbasics.com
e-mail – info@designbasics.com

Chief Executive Officer	Dennis Brozak
President	Linda Reimer
Director of Marketing	Kevin Blair
Business Development	Paul Foresman
Controller	Janie Murnane
Editor-in-Chief	Bruce Arant

Text and Design © 2000 by Design Basics Inc.
All rights reserved.

Cover Photo: plan 2261 Arant

Builder: Webb Building & Development

design basics inc.
HOME PLAN DESIGN SERVICE

library of congress
control number: 00-133411

ISBN: 1-892150-22-0

special places

It seems that more than ever, we're looking for ways to focus on the things we value most. So is it any wonder that we're spending more time at home? A natural outcome of this is an emphasis on discovering "special places" in the home which add comfort, convenience and points of personal refuge.

With entrepreneurs, freelancers and telecommuters working at home in record numbers, home offices have become tremendously popular. Even if we don't work at home, we generally own a "family" computer. Having separate computer areas with room for software, reference books, games and supplies keeps everything organized. Likewise, those of us who like to do our own gardening, decorating projects or repairs, appreciate a designated work space in the home.

The desire to put family first has increased our demand for finished basements and hearth rooms where we can gather together. At the same time, our hectic lifestyles

special places to:

Gather: a comfortable, cozy hearth room. (left)

Get Away: the quiet solitude of a master suite sitting room. (top)

Work: a home office for getting down to business. (middle)

Use However You Choose: flexible space in a finished room over the garage. (bottom)
Photo by: John Stockwell

Play: keeping the rest of the home tidy—a playroom for the kids. (right)

are refreshed by "get-away" rooms. Dens, sitting rooms and sun rooms allow us to take "mini-vacations," or escape for brief retreats without leaving home.

We're also finding more time for recreation by cutting down on driving time. That often translates into having special places to "play" — a hobby room where our individual pastimes can be pursued, or an exercise room to eliminate the need to go to a gym (and wait to use the equipment). Those of us with young children appreciate play rooms where our children can play safely in a place that's designed to get messy.

Whether it's a longing for permanence in a rapidly changing world, or roots that have grown deep from spending more time at home, many of us are looking for homes we can stay in long-term. For that reason, we may look for homes that have flexible spaces that can change as our needs change: lofts which can be used as a play room, a computer area or a den; a finished room over the garage which can be a game room and later converted to a home office.

A STUDY OF HOME™ ~ special places presents one-hundred home designs with unique areas which beckon us to spend more time at home. In addition to these designs, you'll discover ideas you may want to consider in planning your own special places. It's our hope that A STUDY OF HOME™ ~ special places will help you find a design you'll love to come home to, with special places you'll hate to leave.

special places to Work

This home office is shown for example purposes only and is not from the patagonia.

home offices

Thirty years ago, a "home office" was likely a designated corner of an unfinished basement with a file cabinet next to a typewriter sitting on a tacky green, metal stand. It was the spot where term papers were typed, bills were paid and tax records were filed. Today, with more and more Americans bringing work home or working at home full-time, the home office has become very important. The following tips will help make it a comfortable, efficient area to work in.

• If the office will receive regular outside traffic from clients or deliveries, you may want a separate entrance or to have the office located near the front door. (Check your neighborhood's zoning for restrictions.)

• Plan to have proper lighting. Blinds provide the most choices in natural light control. Several small low-intensity light fixtures rather than one large high-intensity light overhead are usually better. This also creates a more inviting atmosphere.

• Discuss your needs for special wiring, phone lines and computer cables with your builder. You may want to add a separate electrical circuit. If you plan to use a modem or fax machine frequently, you will probably want to install a separate telephone line. A surge protector is essential. And a special wire management system to hide unsightly wires is a nice addition.

www.designbasics.com

the patagonia

#50A~5086

price code 24

Located just inside the front door, this study offers easy access to visitors and privacy from the main living areas.

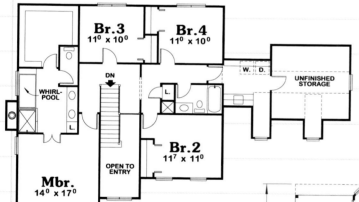

Br.3
11^0 x 10^0

Br.4
11^0 x 10^0

WHIRL-POOL

DN

W. D.

UNFINISHED STORAGE

L.

Mbr.
14^0 x 17^0

OPEN TO ENTRY

Br.2
11^7 x 11^0

Unfinished Storage
Adds 198 Sq. Ft.

1162 main floor
1255 second floor

2417 total sq. ft.

NOTE: 9 ft. main level walls

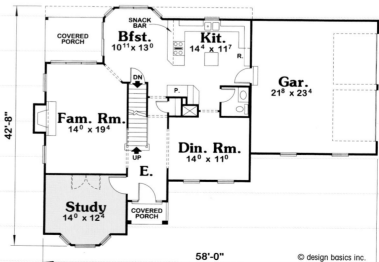

COVERED PORCH

SNACK BAR

Bfst.
10^{11} x 13^0

Kit.
14^4 x 11^7

R.

Gar.
21^8 x 23^4

DN

42'-8"

Fam. Rm.
14^0 x 19^4

P.

UP

Din. Rm.
14^0 x 11^0

E.

Study
14^0 x 12^4

COVERED PORCH

58'-0"

© design basics inc.

the holden

#50A~4998

price code 22

2227 total sq. ft.

NOTE: 9 ft. main level walls

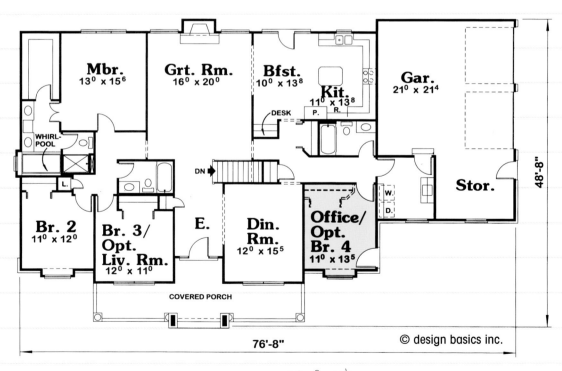

With its own outside entrance in the front
of the home, this office is ideal for someone
who meets with clients or vendors.

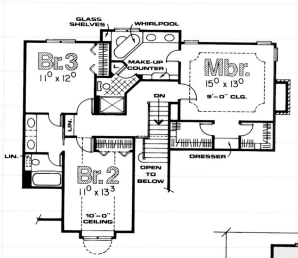

the lawler

#50A~2898   price code 24

Located on a secluded wing with its own outside entrance, this home office won't interfere with family life.

1535   main floor
962   second floor
2497   total sq. ft.

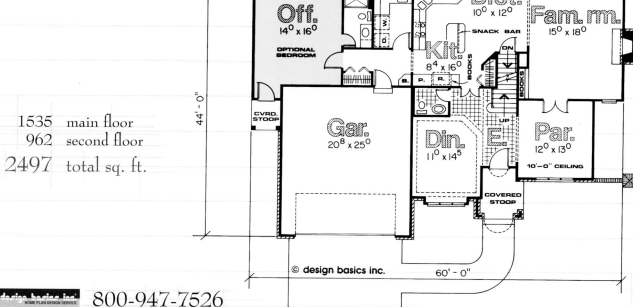

© design basics inc.

the briarwood

#50A~2956   price code 25

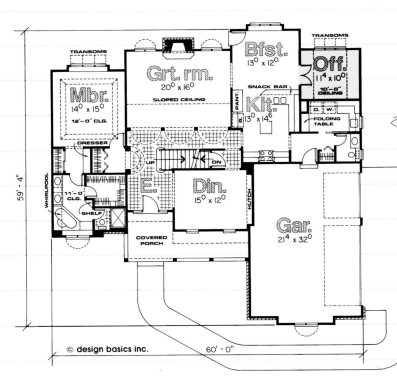

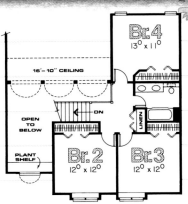

French doors, transom-topped windows and a sloped ceiling make working in this home office more pleasant.

1875	main floor
687	second floor
2562	total sq. ft.

computer spaces

Unlike the home office, a computer area is generally used by the entire family for homework, games and household management. It's often centrally located to provide convenient access for everyone—in a loft, in a finished basement or a built-in desk in the kitchen. To get the most from this area of your home, you'll want to consider lighting, ergonomics and storage space for supplies, software and games.

#50A~24041
price code 39

the lagoda

This computer space is shown for example purposes only and is not from the lagoda.

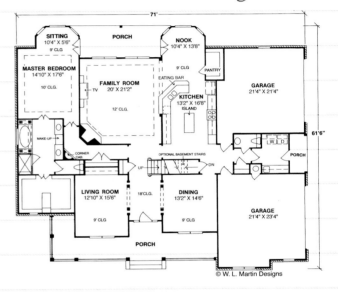

© W. L. Martin Designs

2472   main floor
1442   second floor
3914   total sq. ft.

a roomy computer center near three secondary bedrooms will be a popular spot for homework or games.

the calabretta

#50A~4106

price code 26

1333	main floor
1280	second floor
2613	total sq. ft.

NOTE: 9 ft. main level walls

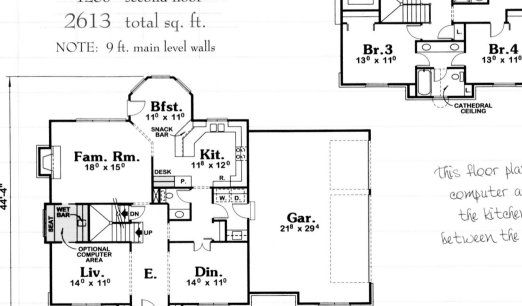

WHIRLPOOL TUB

CATHEDRAL CEILING

Mbr.
15⁰ x 15⁰

9'-0" CEILING

Br.2
12⁰ x 12⁰

DN

Unfinished Bonus
21⁸ x 14⁰

Br.3
13⁰ x 11⁰

Br.4
13⁰ x 11⁰

CATHEDRAL CEILING

Unfinished Future Space
Adds 323 Sq. Ft.

Bfst.
11⁰ x 11⁰

SNACK BAR

Fam. Rm.
18⁰ x 15⁰

Kit.
11⁸ x 12⁰

DESK

P.

R.

W. D.

SEAT

WET BAR

DN

UP

OPTIONAL COMPUTER AREA

Liv.
14⁰ x 11⁰

E.

Din.
14⁰ x 11⁰

Gar.
21⁸ x 29⁴

44'-4"

STOOP

58'-0"

© design basics inc.

This floor plan offers two options for computer areas - a built-in desk off the kitchen or a walk-thru area between the family and living rooms.

the hanna

#50A~4081   price code 25

a centrally located desk on the second floor is a convenient spot for a computer.

OPEN TO BELOW
19'-0" CEILING
DESK
Br.3 13³ x 12⁰
Br.2 14⁰ x 13⁰
OPTIONAL STUDY
BOOKS   BOOKS
Br.4 13³ x 11⁰
DN
L.
L.

WHIRLPOOL TUB
L.
Grt. Rm. 16⁰ x 17¹⁰
19'-0" CEILING
CATHEDRAL CEILING
ENTERT. CENTER
Bfst. 10⁸ x 16⁰
Kit. 11⁰ x 12⁰
SNACK BAR
P.   R.   P.
DN
UP
W.   D.
Din. 14⁰ x 13⁰
E.
Mbr. 14⁰ x 15²
10'-4" CEILING
BOOKS   BOOKS
CURIO   CURIO
STOOP
Gar. 22⁰ x 23⁰

54'-0"
58'-8"
© design basics inc.

1735   main floor
841   second floor
2576   total sq. ft.
NOTE: 9 ft. main level walls

work spaces

Whether the task is potting plants, building models, woodworking, refinishing furniture, or repairing and restoring automobiles, handy people need handy places to work. Using perforated hardboard for a board and peg system is a simple way to hang frequently used tools. Enclosed cabinets keep sharp tools away from children and keep the area looking tidy. Task lighting directly on the work surface is a necessity for detail work.

#50A~3010
price code 14

the quimby

This work space is shown for example purposes only and is not from the quimby.

this garage offers two options for workspaces — an indented spot for a workbench on the left or a larger area in the back.

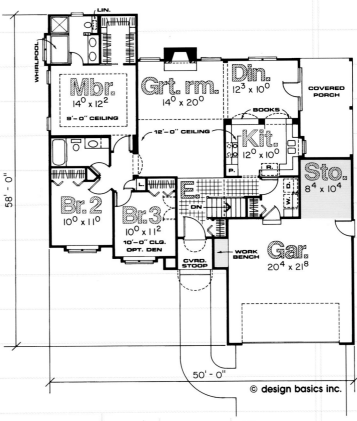

1422 total sq. ft.

www.designbasics.com

the briar manor

#50A~9207   price code 23

2331   total sq. ft.

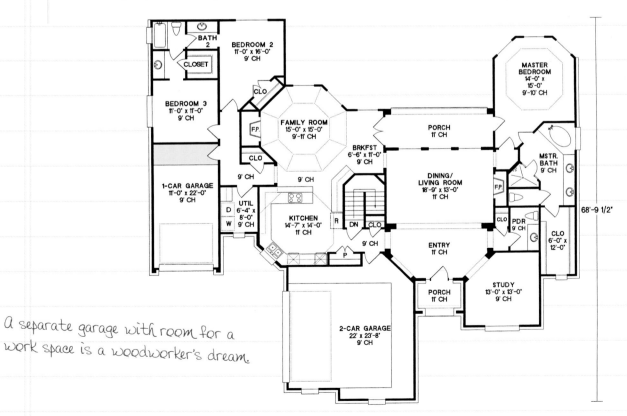

*A separate garage with room for a
work space is a woodworker's dream.*

© CARMICHAEL & DAME DESIGNS, INC.

the stonelake manor

#50A~9200   price code 26

Windows on two sides and an 11-foot ceiling would make a pleasant workspace.

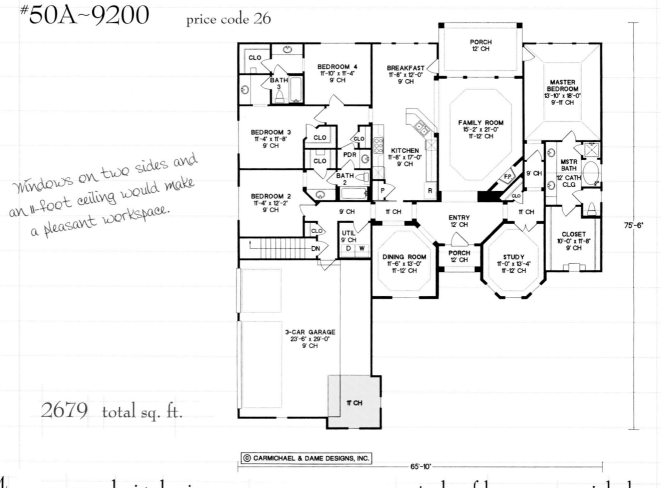

2679 total sq. ft.

the hartley

#50A~2949   price code 24

An indented area in this garage
is the perfect spot for a workbench

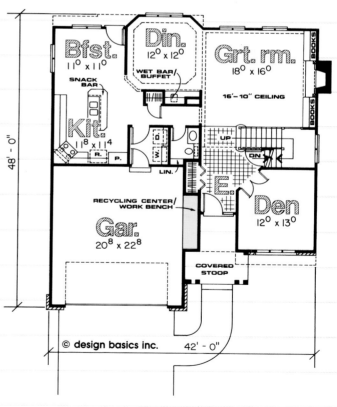

Bfst.
11⁰ x 11⁰

Din.
12⁰ x 12⁰

WET BAR/ BUFFET

Grt. rm.
18⁰ x 16⁰

BOOKS

16'-10" CEILING

SNACK BAR

Kit.
11⁸ x 11⁴

R.   P.

W
D

LIN.

UP

DN

48' - 0"

RECYCLING CENTER/ WORK BENCH

Gar.
20⁸ x 22⁸

E.

Den
12⁰ x 13⁰

COVERED STOOP

© design basics inc.   42' - 0"

Mbr.
16⁰ x 13⁰

CATHEDRAL CEILING

OPEN TO GREAT ROOM

16'-10" CEILING

WHIRLPOOL

11'-0" CLG.

L

DRESSER

SEAT

LIN.

DN

Br. 2
11⁸ x 12⁰

DESK

Br. 3
11⁰ x 13⁰

Br. 4
12⁰ x 12⁶

11'-8" CLG.

SEAT

1216   main floor
1188   second floor
2404   total sq. ft.

design basics inc.
HOME PLAN DESIGN SERVICE

800-947-7526

15

special places to Play

This hobby room is shown for example purposes only and is not from the crescent court.

hobby rooms

Having a separate, organized room allows hobbyists to make the most of small amounts of spare time without feeling rushed to complete a project. Consider the seamstress who must drag out a portable sewing machine, set it up on the dining room table, cut out fabric on the living room floor and then hurry to finish the project so the household can return to normal. What a difference a sewing room could make. Here are some things to think about while planning a hobby room:

• Storage will need to be individualized. Sewing will require a system for keeping threads tidy, ample cupboards for fabrics and a convenient ironing board.

• If there are children in the home, a cabinet which locks is important for woodworking tools or toxic artists' supplies. A photographer will require an organized system for safely storing an ever-growing number of pictures.

• Easy-to-clean surfaces on the counters and floor and a sink for washing up are practical additions for "messy" hobbies.

• If loud equipment will be used, acoustical tile and extra insulation in the walls can reduce noise in the rest of the home.

• Extra ventilation may be required for using a kiln, lacquers or glues.

the crescent court

#50A~9191   price code 23

2393 total sq. ft.

Unfinished Future Room
Adds 222 Sq. Ft.

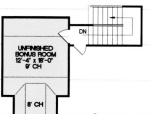

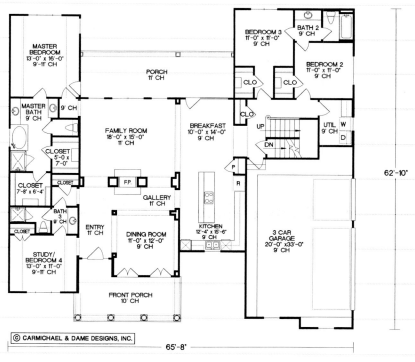

On a separate level from the rest of the home, this unfinished bonus room would be the perfect spot for a "messy" hobby.

the taylor

#50A~3063   price code 19

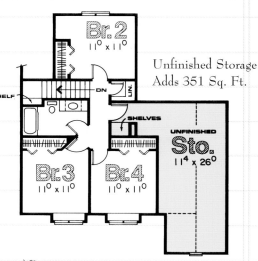

Unfinished Storage
Adds 351 Sq. Ft.

this unfinished storage area adds 351 square feet - perfect for a hobby like painting which requires a lot of room.

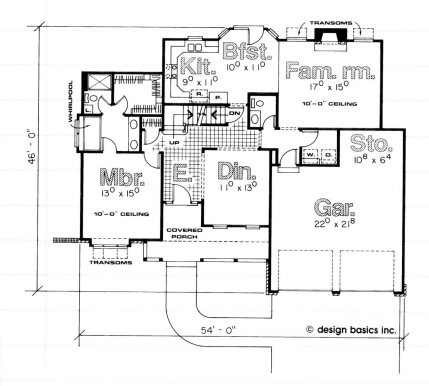

1348   main floor
609   second floor
1957   total sq. ft.

the gerard

#50A~4135

price code 23

Fam. Rm.
18⁰ x 14⁰

Bfst.
11⁰ x 10⁰

Kit.
10⁰ x 12⁸

WET
BAR

P.   R.

DN

UP

Liv. Rm.
11⁰ x 14⁰

E.

**Din.
Rm.**
10⁴ x 13⁶

Gar.
20⁸ x 22⁰

COVERED
STOOP

D   W

44'-0"

50'-0"

© design basics inc.

Mbr.
15⁰ x 14⁰

9'-0" CEILING

Br. 2
11⁰ x 12⁸

DN

L.

Br. 3
11⁰ x 12⁰

Br. 4
10⁰ x 13¹⁰

UNFINISHED
STORAGE

Unfinished Storage
Adds 247 Sq. Ft.

*the bend in this space
over the garage could
subtly divide the room
for multiple hobbies.*

1199   main floor
1150   second floor

2349   total sq. ft.

NOTE: 9 ft. main level walls

HOME PLAN DESIGN SERVICE   800-947-7526

19

playrooms

Children master the world through play. By having a room where they're free to make messes, be noisy and have fun, they learn and grow and make endless happy memories. Having a separate room for play reserves bedrooms for peaceful activities such as reading and sleeping and encourages children to share and get along. Play rooms don't have to be elaborate, but some simple ideas can make them more practical.

• Covering a wall with cork or fabric-wrapped fiberboard will provide plenty of room to display projects. Choose a strong fabric such as denim or burlap which won't ravel.

• Blackboards never seem to go out of style. Create your own by applying two or three coats of special blackboard paint to any smooth surface. (If you're using wood, prime first.) Attach concave picture molding at the bottom to hold chalk and catch dust.

• Organized storage is a must, with plenty of shelves, bins, boxes and baskets. Toy chests with wheels make pickups quicker. If the chest has a lid, make sure it has a safety hinge.

#50A~24011
price code 26

the oliver

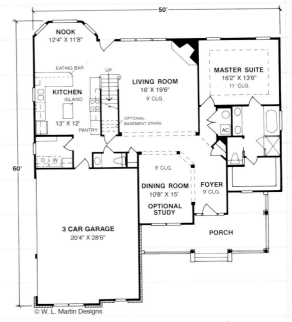

© W. L. Martin Designs

Open to the hall space, the oliver's playroom seems even larger than it is.

This playroom is shown for example purposes only and is not from the oliver.

...happily ever after!

1650 main floor
1038 second floor
2688 total sq. ft.

www.designbasics.com

the meadow creek

#50A~8077   price code 18

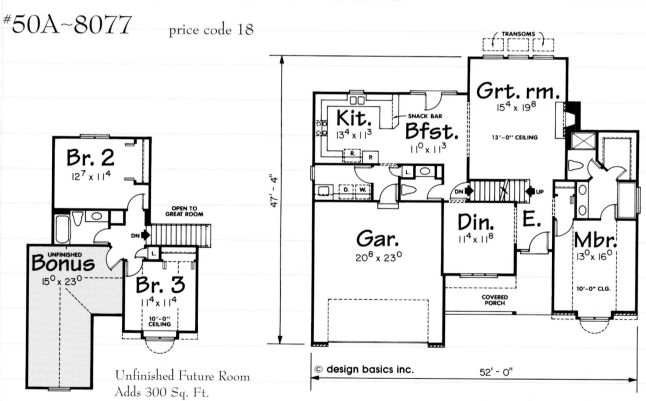

Unfinished Future Room
Adds 300 Sq. Ft.

*this spacious area close to the kids' rooms
would make a perfect playroom*

1405	main floor
453	second floor
1858	total sq. ft.

design basics inc.
HOME PLAN DESIGN SERVICE

the pembrook

#50A~24007   price code 29

A combined play room and study area gives children the best of both worlds.

2101   main floor
877   second floor
2978   total sq. ft.

a study of home ~ special places

the sycamore

#50A~6715   price code 14

Set apart from other family living areas, this unfinished area would be a great place for kids to play without disturbing others.

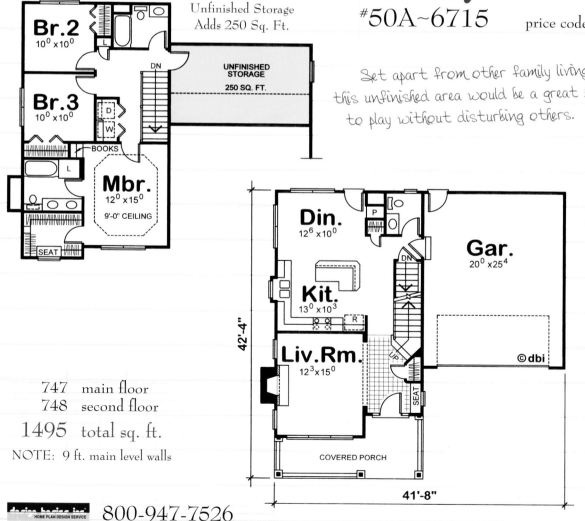

Br.2 10⁰ x 10⁰

Br.3 10⁰ x 10⁰

D
W

BOOKS

Mbr. 12⁰ x 15⁰
9'-0" CEILING

L

SEAT

Unfinished Storage Adds 250 Sq. Ft.

DN

UNFINISHED STORAGE
250 SQ. FT.

Din. 12⁶ x 10⁰

P

Kit. 13⁰ x 10³

R

Gar. 20⁰ x 25⁴

DN

Liv.Rm. 12³ x 15⁰

UP

SEAT

©dbi

42'-4"

COVERED PORCH

41'-8"

747   main floor
748   second floor
1495   total sq. ft.
NOTE: 9 ft. main level walls

HOME PLAN DESIGN SERVICE

exercise rooms

Many of us are more likely to exercise if we have a convenient space designed specifically for the purpose. For most physical activities tough, durable flooring is most practical - vinyl and rubber tile are good choices. If you plan to do aerobics, you may want to consider a special wood flooring system with "give" in it. A thick rubber mat is a plus for lifting weights or doing stretches. You may also want to make provisions for a television or stereo in the room.

This exercise room is shown for example purposes only and is not from the angel cove.

#50A~8094
price code 17

the angel cove

The angel cove's second floor bonus room could easily accommodate a treadmill, rowing machine and a weight system.

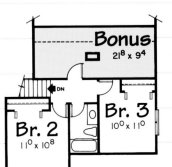

Bonus
21⁸ x 9⁴

Unfinished Future Room
Adds 212 Sq. Ft.

Br. 2
11⁰ x 10⁸

Br. 3
10⁰ x 11⁰

1324   main floor
391   second floor
1715   total sq. ft.

TRANSOMS

Bfst.
11⁴ x 10⁰

SNACK BAR

Mbr.
14⁰ x 13⁰

Grt. rm.
14⁰ x 18⁶

Kit.
11⁴ x 11⁰

10'-5" CEILING

E.

UP   DN

W. D.

Din.
11⁰ x 13⁰

Gar.
19⁴ x 22⁰

TRANSOM

COVERED STOOP

54' - 0"

40' - 8"   © design basics inc.

www.designbasics.com

the summerfield

#50A~6712   price code 19

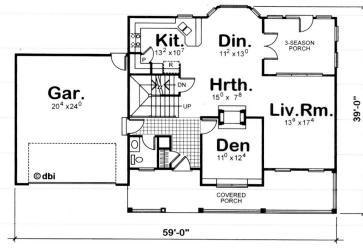

Gar.
20⁴ x24⁰

Kit.
13² x10⁷

Din.
11² x13⁰

3-SEASON PORCH

Hrth.
15⁰ x 7⁸

Liv.Rm.
13⁰ x17⁴

Den
11⁰ x12⁴

COVERED PORCH

39'-0"

59'-0"

©dbi

Located inside the master suite, this unfinished area would make a secluded exercise room.

Unfinished Storage Rooms
Add 402 Sq. Ft.

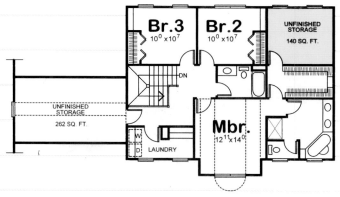

Br.3
10⁰ x10⁷

Br.2
10⁰ x10⁷

UNFINISHED STORAGE
140 SQ. FT.

UNFINISHED STORAGE
262 SQ. FT.

Mbr.
12¹¹x14⁰

LAUNDRY

1015 main floor
945 second floor
1960 total sq. ft.
NOTE: 9 ft. main level walls

special places to Gather

This finished basement is shown for example purposes only and is not from the hawthorne.

finished basements

Not so long ago "finished" basements translated into painted cement block or paneled walls, grid ceilings and rubber backed carpet. Today, they are referred to as lower levels and are true extensions of the home's living spaces. Because they are rather isolated, they're well suited to many uses including entertainment centers, hobby rooms, exercise rooms, home offices, workshops or private apartments for grown children. Before finishing a lower level, you may want to consider:

• If your lot is not suited to a walkout basement, installing window light wells can provide bigger windows. Placing them on the south or southwest side of the home will provide the most light.

• Having your builder add an extra course of blocks or use higher forms for poured walls will make the area feel less like a basement and be well-worth the extra cost in the long run.

• Using engineered wood products allows builders to have greater open spans with less support beams. Engineered wood systems have special openings for running wiring and plumbing through them, eliminating lowered soffits.

www.designbasics.com

cont'd on page 32

the hawthorne

#50A~2799   price code 18

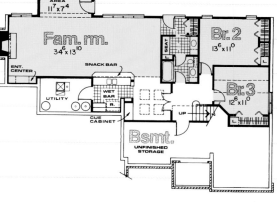

GAME AREA
11⁷x7⁴

Fam. rm.
34⁶x13¹⁰

Br. 2
13⁶x11⁰

Br. 3
12⁶x11⁰

ENT. CENTER

SNACK BAR

SEAT

WET BAR

UTILITY

CUE CABINET

UP

Bsmt.
UNFINISHED STORAGE

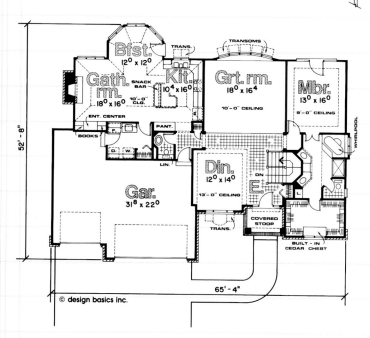

Bfst.
12⁰ x 12⁰

TRANS.

TRANSOMS

Gath. rm.
18⁰ x 16⁰

Kit.
10⁴ x 16⁰

10'-0" CLG.

SNACK BAR

Grt. rm.
18⁰ x 16⁴

10'-0" CEILING

Mbr.
13⁰ x 16⁰

9'-0" CEILING

ENT. CENTER

BOOKS

PANT.

Din.
12⁰ x 14⁰

13'-0" CEILING

LIN.

Gar.
31⁸ x 22⁰

WHIRLPOOL

TRANS.

COVERED STOOP

BUILT - IN CEDAR CHEST

52' - 8"

65' - 4"

© design basics inc.

*In addition to an oversized family room
and bayed game area, this lower level includes
two bedrooms and a full size bath.*

1887   total sq. ft.

the fairway

#50A~2651

price code 23

Casual entertaining will be a breeze with this enormous family room and game area and a nearby snack bar and wet bar.

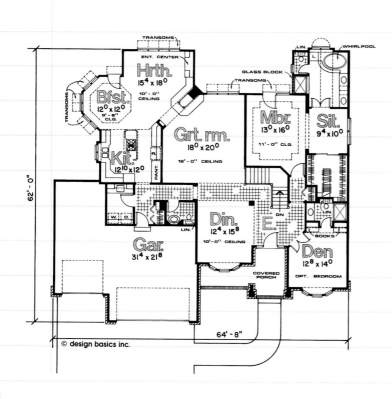

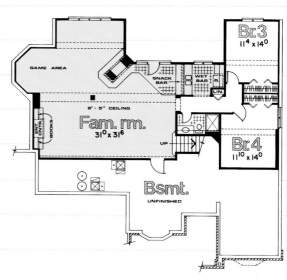

Optional Finished Basement
Adds 1475 Sq. Ft.

2317 total sq. ft.

the payson

#50A~5034   price code 14

1472 total sq. ft.

NOTE: 9 ft. main level walls

Optional Finished Basement Adds 1169 Sq. Ft.

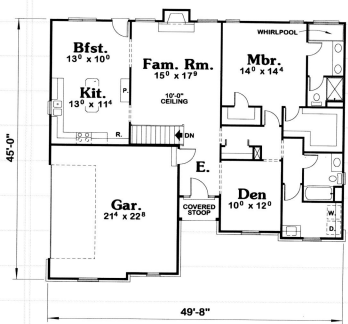

Bfst. 13⁰ x 10⁰

Kit. 13⁰ x 11⁴

Fam. Rm. 15⁰ x 17⁹   10'-0" CEILING

Mbr. 14⁰ x 14⁴   WHIRLPOOL

P.   R.   DN   E.

Den 10⁰ x 12⁰

COVERED STOOP   W. D.

Gar. 21⁴ x 22⁸

45'-0"

49'-8"

This lower level family room features a corner fireplace, built-in entertainment center and a small kitchen.

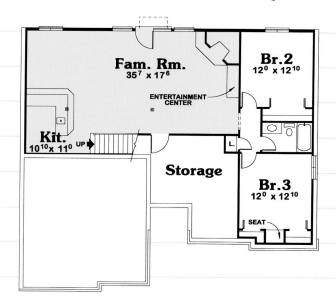

Fam. Rm. 35⁷ x 17⁶

ENTERTAINMENT CENTER

Kit. 10¹⁰ x 11⁰   UP

Storage

Br.2 12⁰ x 12¹⁰

Br.3 12⁰ x 12¹⁰

SEAT

the stonybrook

#50A~3578   price code 15

1595 total sq. ft.

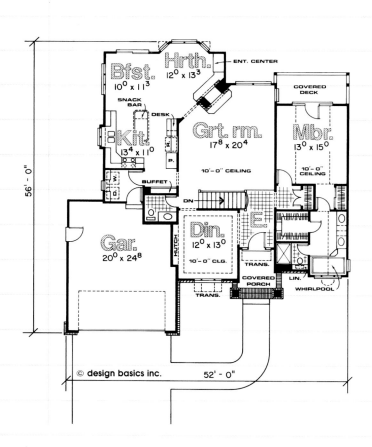

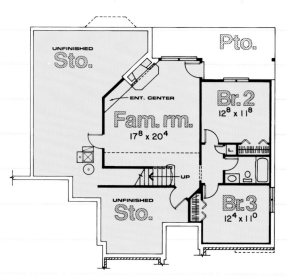

Optional Finished Basement
Adds 790 Sq. Ft.

*a charming family room, extra
bedrooms and ample storage are included
in this lower level floor plan*

30   www.designbasics.com   a study of home ~ special places

the richardson

#50A~3303

price code 20

2083 total sq. ft.

NOTE: 9 ft. main level walls

two roomy bedrooms with walk-in closets, a spacious family room and a kitchenette make the most of this home's lower level.

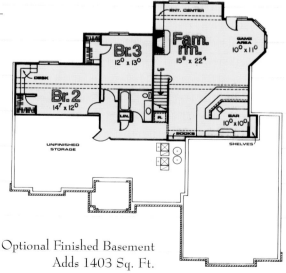

Optional Finished Basement
Adds 1403 Sq. Ft.

800-947-7526

This finished basement is shown for example purposes only.

• Incorporate support beams into walls dividing rooms or open shelving units, or turn them into architectural assets by building pillars or columns around them.

• The most economical time to correct a radon problem is before the basement is finished. Tests to check radon levels are available at hardware stores and home supply centers.

• Be sure the basement is completely waterproof before finishing it. Check the grading to make sure it slopes away from the foundation. If the water table is high, a sump pump should be installed. It's a good idea to seal the floor with an epoxy sealer and cover the walls with concrete paint.

• Although wood flooring is not recommended for below grade installations, laminate plank works well because it's resistant to moisture. Since planks are glued to each other (not directly fastened to the subfloor) and sit on a cushioned backing, small cracks and imperfections in the cement won't matter.

• If the ceiling will be sheetrocked (instead of acoustical tiles), it's important to provide adequate power outlets and to prewire for media speakers. It will be much harder to add wiring after the ceiling and walls are closed.

www.designbasics.com

#50A~1179

price code 20

sawyer

This built-in desk in the breakfast area would make a convenient computer area for the whole family.

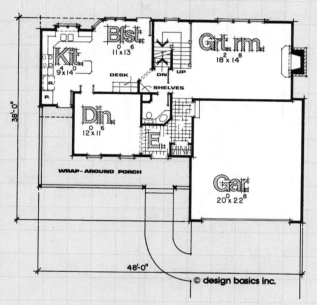

Bfst. 11 x 13

Kit. 9 x 14

Grt. rm. 18 x 14

DESK

SHELVES

UP

DN

Din. 12 x 11

E.

WRAP-AROUND PORCH

Gar. 20 x 22⁸

38'-0"

48'-0"

© design basics inc.

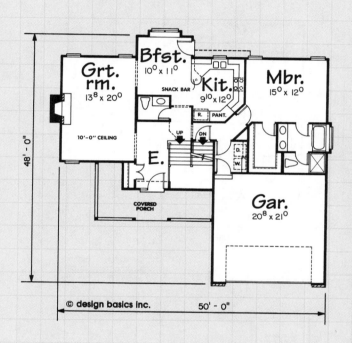

Grt. rm. 13⁸ x 20⁰

Bfst. 10⁰ x 11⁰

SNACK BAR

Kit. 9¹⁰ x 12⁰

Mbr. 15⁰ x 12⁰

10'-0" CEILING

R. PANT.

UP

DN

D.

W.

E.

COVERED PORCH

Gar. 20⁸ x 21⁰

48'-0"

50'-0"

© design basics inc.

Br. 12 x 10⁴

DN

Mbr. 15 x 13

D.

W.

Br. 11 x 11⁰

Br. 11 x 11

LIN.

WHIRL POOL

927   main floor
1163   second floor
2090   total sq. ft.

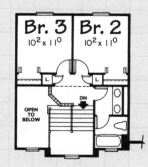

Br. 3 10² x 11⁰

Br. 2 10² x 11⁰

OPEN TO BELOW

DN

1210   main floor
405   second floor
1615   total sq. ft.

With a lovely boxed window, this breakfast area will provide a great view of the back yard.

#50A~9160
price code 26

woodlands showcase

#50A~1380
price code 19

paterson

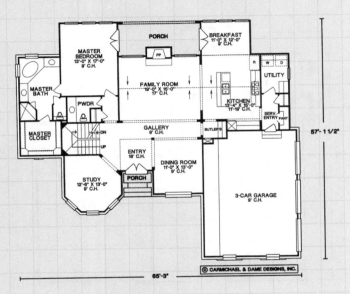

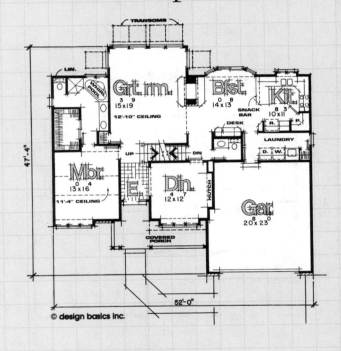

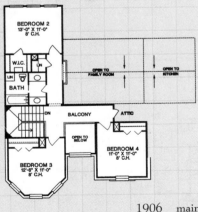

1906   main floor
749   second floor
2655   total sq. ft.

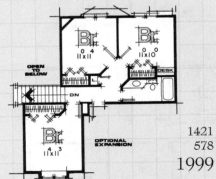

1421   main floor
578   second floor
1999   total sq. ft.

this uniquely shaped study provides a beautiful place for reading or reflection.

In this flexible floor plan a home office could be created in the dining room or the fourth bedroom.

a study of home ~ special places

#50A~8024

price code 22

millard oaks

#50A~6266

price code 28

halstead

Should the need arise, the dining room in the front of the house could also be used as an office.

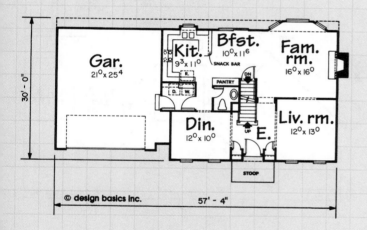

Gar.
21⁰ x 25⁴

Kit.
9³ x 11⁰

Bfst.
10⁰ x 11⁶

SNACK BAR

Fam. rm.
16⁰ x 16⁰

PANTRY

D. W.

R.

Din.
12⁰ x 10⁰

UP E.

Liv. rm.
12⁰ x 13⁰

DN

STOOP

30' - 0"

© design basics inc. 57' - 4"

1000	main floor
1298	second floor
2298	total sq. ft.

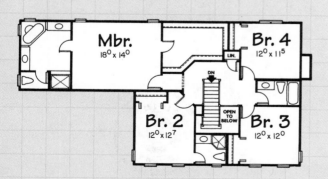

Mbr.
18⁰ x 14⁰

Br. 4
12⁰ x 11⁵

LIN.

DN

OPEN TO BELOW

Br. 2
12⁰ x 12⁷

Br. 3
12⁰ x 12⁰

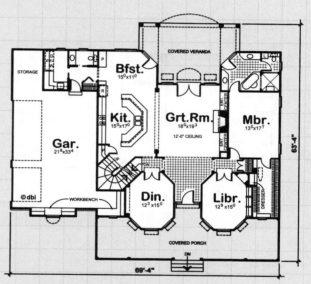

STORAGE

Bfst.
15⁰ x 11⁰

Gar.
21⁶ x 33⁴

Kit.
15⁰ x 17⁰

COVERED VERANDA

Grt. Rm.
18⁰ x 19³
12'-0" CEILING

Mbr.
13⁰ x 17⁷

UP

DN

WORKBENCH

© dbi

Din.
12³ x 15⁰

Libr.
12⁹ x 15⁰

DRESSER

COVERED PORCH

DN

69'-4"

63' - 4"

What reader wouldn't love this octagon-shaped library with built-in bookcases?

Unfinished Storage Adds 1023 Sq. Ft.

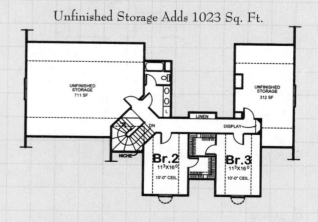

UNFINISHED STORAGE 711 SF

UNFINISHED STORAGE 312 SF

LINEN

DISPLAY

DN

NICHE

Br. 2
11³ x 16⁰
10'-0" CEIL.

Br. 3
11³ X 16⁰
10'-0" CEIL.

2092	main floor
728	second floor
2820	total sq. ft.

NOTE: 9 ft. main level walls

#50A~24004
price code 22

bardel

#50A~4208
price code 20

creighton

© W. L. Martin Designs

1568   main floor
680   second floor
2248   total sq. ft.

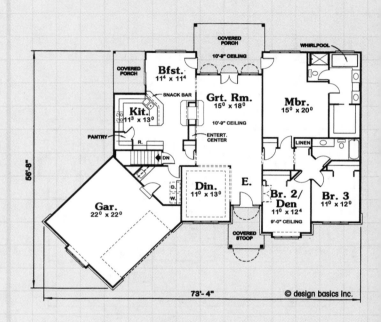

2057   total sq. ft.

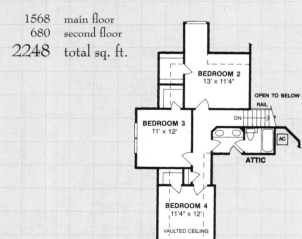

An over-sized master bedroom includes an adjoining sitting area with access to a covered porch.

Adjoining the dining room, a walk-in pantry and a butler's pantry simplify entertaining.

a study of home ~ special places

#50A~24019
price code 38

belmont

An octagon-shaped sitting area with bayed windows and special ceiling detail adorns this master bedroom.

SITTING
9'8" X 9'8"

PORCH

NOOK
9'8" X 9'8"

FAMILY ROOM
17 X 20'

EATING BAR

9' CLG.

MASTER BEDROOM
17'6" X 14'6"
9' CLG.

LIVING ROOM
14'8" X 13'6"
14' CLG

KITCHEN
13'2" X 14'

UP

REF

PANTRY

OPTIONAL BASEMENT STAIRS

W D

MASTER BATH

STOR

ARCH

OPEN TO ABOVE

BUTLER'S PANTRY

AC

UP

DINING ROOM
12'8" X 17'2"
9' CLG.

3 CAR GARAGE
21'4" X 29'6"

STUDY
12' x 15'
9' CLG.

© W. L. Martin Designs

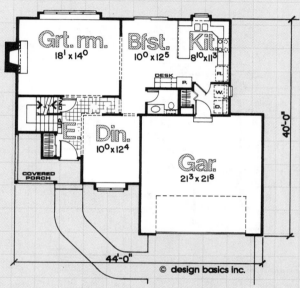

Grt. rm.
18' x 14'0

Bfst.
10'0 x 12'5

Kit.
8'10 x 11'3

DESK

P.

R.

W.

DN

Din.
10'0 x 12'4

Gar.
21'3 x 21'8

COVERED PORCH

40'-0"

44'-0"

© design basics inc.

A computer on the desk in the breakfast area will allow Mom to help children with homework during meal preparation.

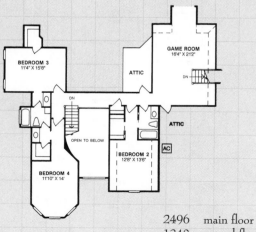

BEDROOM 3
11'4" X 15'8"

GAME ROOM
16'4" X 21'2"

ATTIC

DN

DN

OPEN TO BELOW

ATTIC

BEDROOM 2
12'8" X 13'6"

AC

BEDROOM 4
11'10" X 14'

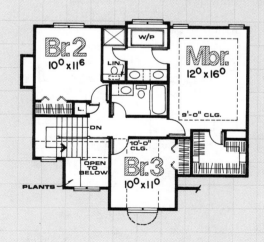

Br. 2
10'0 x 11'6

w/p

Mbr.
12'0 x 16'0

LIN.

L.

8'-0" CLG.

DN

OPEN TO BELOW

10'-0" CLG.

Br. 3
10'0 x 11'0

PLANTS

2496   main floor
1348   second floor
3844   total sq. ft.

891   main floor
759   second floor
1650   total sq. ft.

#50A~2249
price code 31

normandy

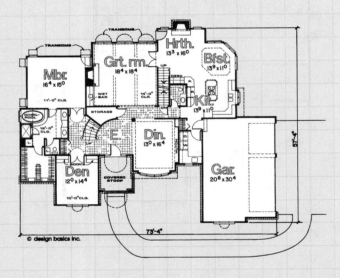

2252 main floor
920 second floor
3172 total sq. ft.

NOTE: 9 ft. main level walls

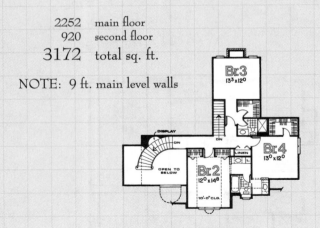

French doors, built-in bookcases and a special arched window enhance this den.

#50A~9161
price code 27

woodvine manor

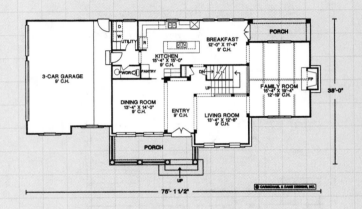

1400 main floor
1315 second floor
2715 total sq. ft.

Smaller families may choose to use the fourth bedroom as a play room.

a study of home ~ special places

#50A~5498

price code 21

hartwell

An adjoining sitting area and access to a private porch turn this master bedroom into a relaxing retreat.

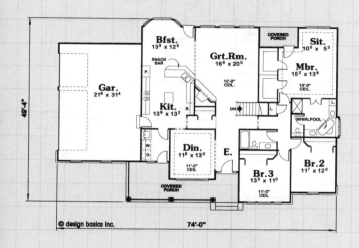

© design basics inc.

2188   total sq. ft.

NOTE: 9 ft. main level walls

#50A~6806

price code 26

san carlos

© design basics inc.

A triple patio door in the great room leads to a screened deck with cathedral ceiling.

2647   total sq. ft.

NOTE: 9 ft. main level walls

#50A~8053
price code 19 **stevens woods**

#50A~2818
price code 16 **orchard**

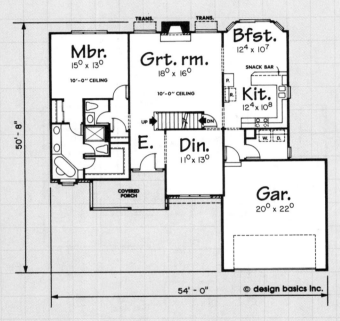

Mbr. 15⁰ x 13⁰
10'-0" CEILING

Grt. rm. 18⁰ x 16⁰
10'-0" CEILING

Bfst. 12⁴ x 10⁷

SNACK BAR

Kit. 12⁴ x 10⁸

TRANS. TRANS.

P.
R.

UP DN

E. Din. 11⁰ x 13⁰

W. D.

COVERED PORCH

Gar. 20⁰ x 22⁰

50'-8"

54'-0"   © design basics inc.

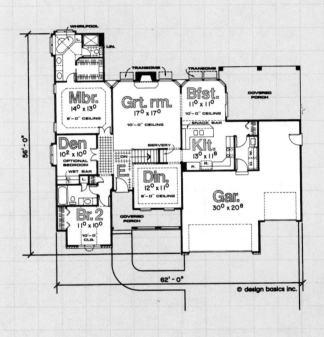

WHIRLPOOL   LIN.

Mbr. 14⁰ x 13⁰
9'-0" CEILING

Grt. rm. 17⁰ x 17⁰
10'-0" CEILING

Bfst. 11⁰ x 11⁰
10'-0" CEILING

COVERED PORCH

Den 10² x 10⁰
OPTIONAL BEDROOM

WET BAR

SERVERY

Kit. 13⁰ x 11⁸

TRANSOME   TRANSOME

DN

E.

Din. 12⁰ x 11⁰
9'-0" CEILING

P.

W

Br. 2 11⁰ x 10⁰
10'-0" CLG.

COVERED PORCH

Gar. 30⁰ x 20⁸

56'-0"

62'-0"   © design basics inc.

1398 main floor
598 second floor
1996 total sq. ft.

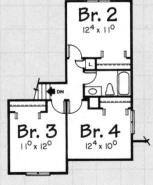

Br. 2 12⁴ x 11⁰

L

DN

Br. 3 11⁰ x 12⁰   Br. 4 12⁴ x 10⁰

1651 total sq. ft.

Br. 3 10⁰ x 10⁰

OPTIONAL BEDROOM

Conveniently located near the master suite, this den features a lovely boxed window and a wet bar.

Families with fewer children may use the fourth bedroom as a flex room for hobbies, exercise or computer work.

a study of home ~ special places

monterey

#50A~9197

price code 23

eldridge court

Three sets of French doors lead to a private porch in the back of the home.

PORCH
9' CH

2 STORY
FAMILY ROOM
19'-2" X 14'-10"
16' CH

KITCHEN
9' CH
10'-0" X
15'-0"

BREAKFAST
11'-0" X 13'-0"
9' CH

UP

FP.

UTILITY
9' CH

CLO

PWD
9' CH

DINING ROOM
11'-0" X 13'-8"
9' CH

ENTRY
9' CH

CLO

DN

STORAGE

R   P

DW

2-CAR
GARAGE
21'-0" X 21'-7"
8' CH

PORCH
9' CH

© CARMICHAEL & DAME DESIGNS, INC.

52'-6"

45'-4"

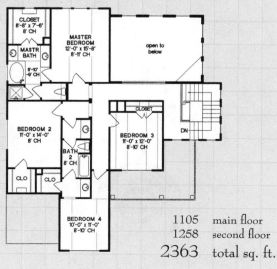

CLOSET
8'-8" X 7'-6"
8' CH

MASTR
BATH

8'-10" X
9' CH

MASTER
BEDROOM
12'-0" X 15'-8"
8'-11"

open to
below

BEDROOM 2
11'-0" X 14'-0"
8' CH

BATH
2
8' CH

CLOSET

BEDROOM 3
11'-0" X 12'-0"
8'-10" CH

DN

CLO   CLO

BEDROOM 4
10'-0" X 11'-0"
8'-10" CH

1105   main floor
1258   second floor
2363   total sq. ft.

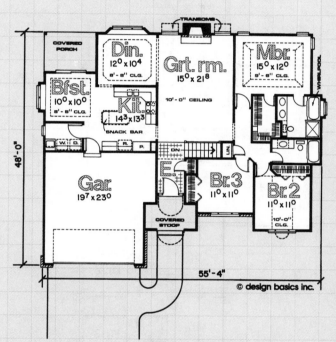

COVERED
PORCH

TRANSOMS

Din.
12⁰ x 10⁴
8'-8" CLG.

Grt. rm.
15⁰ x 21⁸
10'-0" CEILING

Mbr.
15⁰ x 12⁰
9'-8" CLG.

WHIRLPOOL

Bfst.
10⁰ x 10⁰
8'-8" CLG.

Kit.
14³ x 13³

SNACK BAR

W.D.

R   P

DN

LIN.

Gar.
19⁷ x 23⁰

Br. 3
11⁰ x 11⁰

Br. 2
11⁰ x 11⁰
10'-0"
CLG.

COVERED
STOOP

48'-0"

55'-4"

© design basics inc.

1666   total sq. ft.

An extended area in the garage is custom made for a work bench.

#50A~6273
price code 20

st. charles

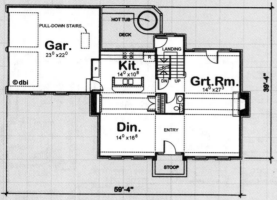

Unfinished Storage
Adds 345 Sq. Ft.

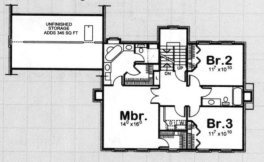

Unfinished Attic
Adds 576 Sq. Ft.

1060 main floor
960 second floor
2020 total sq. ft.

NOTE: 9 ft. main level walls

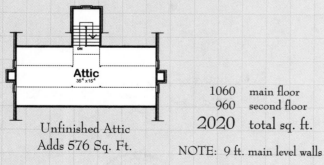

This home is loaded with extras - a deck with hot tub, an unfinished storage area above the garage and a large attic.

#50A~8069
price code 17

quail hollow

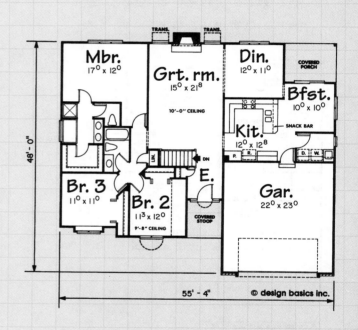

1729 total sq. ft.

Sliding doors off the breakfast area lead to a secluded porch.

#50A~9167
price code 29

stillwater court

#50A~2311
price code 24

pinehurst

A lengthy porch in the back of the home
is entered from the master bedroom,
the breakfast area and the powder room.

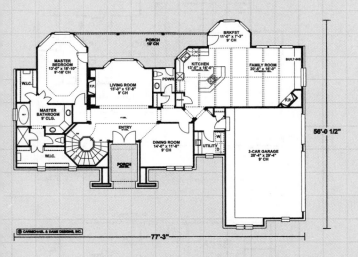

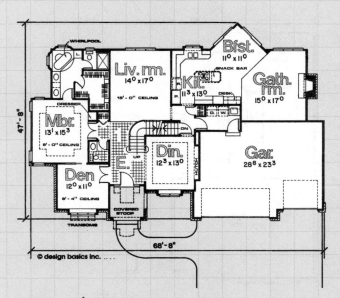

French doors off the entry lead to
a stylish den also accessed through a
pocket door in the master bedroom.

2044	main floor
917	second floor
2961	total sq. ft.

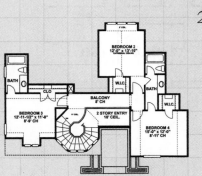

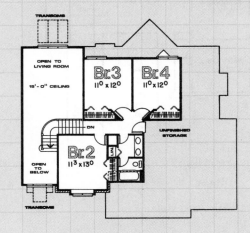

1829	main floor
657	second floor
2486	total sq. ft.

#50A~24022
price code 25

formosa

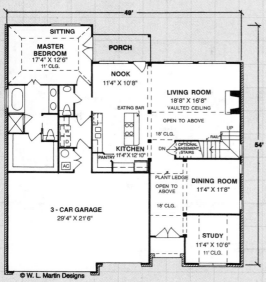

SITTING

MASTER BEDROOM
17'4" X 12'6"
11' CLG.

PORCH

NOOK
11'4" X 10'8"

LIVING ROOM
18'8" X 16'8"
VAULTED CEILING

EATING BAR

OPEN TO ABOVE

18' CLG.

KITCHEN
11'4" X 12'10"

PANTRY

AC

OPTIONAL BASEMENT STAIRS

DN

RAIL

UP

3 - CAR GARAGE
29'4" X 21'6"

PLANT LEDGE
OPEN TO ABOVE
18' CLG.

DINING ROOM
11'4" X 11'8"

STUDY
11'4" X 10'6"
11' CLG.

49'

54'

© W. L. Martin Designs

GAME ROOM
17'6" X 17'4"

OPEN TO BELOW

RAILING

DN

BEDROOM 4
11'6" X 11'

PLANT LEDGE

OPEN TO BELOW

BEDROOM 3
11'6" X 10'6"

AC   ATTIC

BEDROOM 2
10'8" X 13'

PLANT LEDGE

1623   main floor
952   second floor
2575   total sq. ft.

NOTE: 9 ft. main level walls

the whole family will enjoy the oversized game room on the second floor.

44

#50A~5502
price code 21

ridgeville

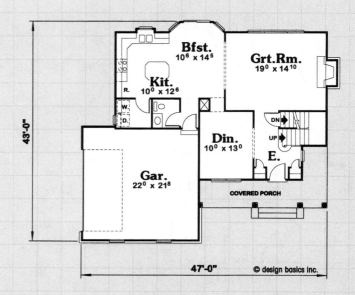

Bfst.
10'6 X 14'6

Grt.Rm.
19'0 X 14'10

Kit.
10'0 X 12'6

R.

W.
D.

DN

UP

Din.
10'0 X 13'0

E.

Gar.
22'0 X 21'8

COVERED PORCH

43'-0"

47'-0"   © design basics inc.

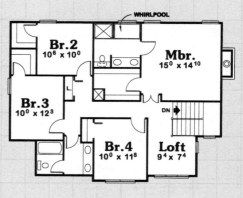

WHIRLPOOL

Br.2
10'6 X 10'0

Mbr.
15'0 X 14'10

Br.3
10'0 X 12'3

DN

Br.4
10'0 X 11'8

Loft
9'4 X 7'4

1006   main floor
1099   second floor
2105   total sq. ft.

NOTE: 9 ft. main level walls

this cozy loft area is the perfect spot for a comfortable easy chair, floor lamp and small bookca

a study of home ~ special places

#50A~24027

price code 21

oakland

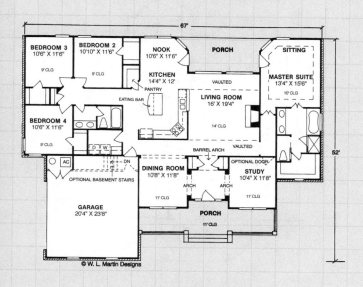

- BEDROOM 3 10'6" X 11'6" — 9' CLG
- BEDROOM 2 10'10" X 11'6" — 9' CLG
- NOOK 10'6" X 11'6"
- PORCH
- SITTING
- KITCHEN 14'4" X 12
- VAULTED
- MASTER SUITE 13'4" X 15'6" — 10' CLG
- PANTRY
- EATING BAR
- BEDROOM 4 10'6" X 11'6" — 9' CLG
- LIVING ROOM 16' X 19'4" — 14' CLG
- BARREL ARCH
- VAULTED
- AC
- OPTIONAL BASEMENT STAIRS
- DINING ROOM 10'8" X 11'8" — 11' CLG
- OPTIONAL DOOR
- STUDY 10'4" X 11'8" — 11' CLG
- ARCH
- ARCH
- GARAGE 20'4" X 23'8"
- PORCH — 11' CLG
- 67'
- 52'

© W. L. Martin Designs

2144 total sq. ft.

the entry offers lovely, arched views in several directions.

#50A~2346

price code 24

fayette

the den in the front of this home features a large, boxed window, a built-in bookcase and angled french doors.

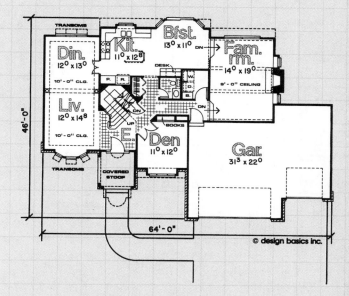

- TRANSOMS
- Din. 12⁰ x 13⁰ — 10'-0" CLG.
- Kit. 11⁰ x 12⁸
- Bfst. 13⁰ x 11⁰
- Fam. rm. 14⁰ x 19⁰ — 9'-0" CEILING
- DESK
- P.
- R.
- Liv. 12⁰ x 14⁸ — 10'-0" CLG.
- UP
- BOOKS
- DN
- Den 11⁰ x 12⁰
- Gar. 31³ x 22⁰
- TRANSOMS
- COVERED STOOP
- 46'-0"
- 64'-0"
- © design basics inc.

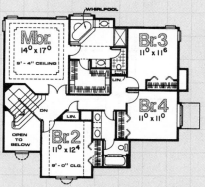

- WHIRLPOOL
- Mbr. 14⁰ x 17⁰ — 9'-4" CEILING
- Br. 3 11⁰ x 11⁶
- LIN.
- Br. 4 11⁰ x 11⁰
- DN
- LIN.
- OPEN TO BELOW
- Br. 2 11⁰ x 12⁴ — 9'-0" CLG.

1369 main floor
1111 second floor
2480 total sq. ft.

design basics inc. HOME PLAN DESIGN SERVICE 800-947-7526

45

#50A~9171
price code 20 **westcott manor**

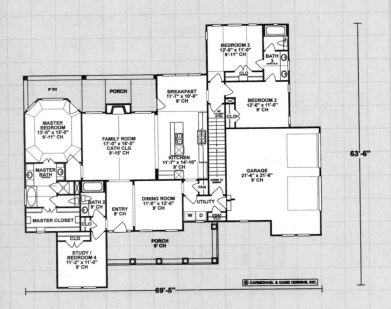

69'-5" · 63'-6"

2040 total sq. ft.

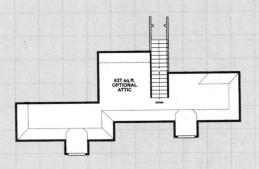

627 sq. ft. OPTIONAL ATTIC

An optional attic provides 627 additional square feet and could be divided into separate areas for different activities.

#50A~2408
price code 22 **crawford**

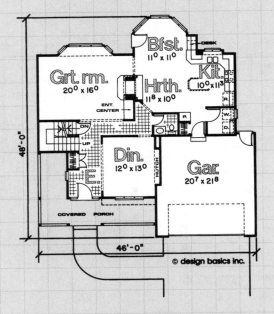

48'-0" · 46'-0"

© design basics inc.

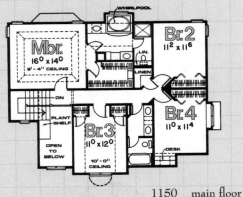

1150 main floor
1120 second floor
2270 total sq. ft.

This cozy hearth room will be a perfect place to enjoy the morning paper and a cup of coffee.

#50A~8090
price code 14

spring valley

Transom-topped windows flank the fireplace in this gracious great room.

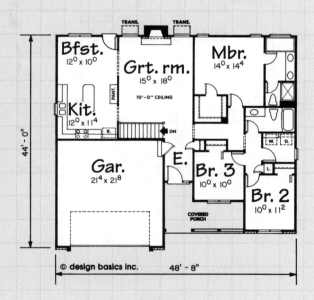

TRANS.   TRANS.

Bfst.
12⁰ x 10⁰

Grt. rm.
15⁰ x 18⁰

Mbr.
14⁰ x 14⁴

10'-0" CEILING

Kit.
12⁰ x 11⁴

PANT.

R.

DN

Gar.
21⁴ x 21⁸

E.

Br. 3
10⁰ x 10⁰

W. D.

L

Br. 2
10⁰ x 11²

COVERED PORCH

44' - 0"

© design basics inc.   48' - 8"

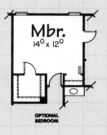

Mbr.
14⁰ x 12⁰

OPTIONAL BEDROOM

1453   total sq. ft.

#50A~2962
price code 23

baldwin

Kit.
10⁰ x 12⁸

Bfst.
11⁴ x 11⁴

Fam. rm.
17⁰ x 15⁰

PANT.

UP

DN

Sto.
9⁸ x 6⁰

W. D.

UP

44' - 0"

Gar.
20⁰ x 22⁰

Din.
11⁰ x 13⁰

E.

Media
12⁰ x 13⁸
ENT. CENTER

TRANS.

TRANS.

COVERED PORCH

© design basics inc.   52' - 8"

Br. 4
10⁰ x 13⁰

Br. 3
11⁰ x 11⁴

Mbr.
13⁰ x 17⁰
9'-4" CEILING

DN

L

LIN.

LIN.

LIN.

OPEN TO BELOW

WHIRLPOOL

Br. 2
11⁰ x 11⁸
10'-0" CLG.

This media room, complete with built-in entertainment center, provides a place for the television away from the family room.

1206   main floor
1171   second floor
2377   total sq. ft.

800-947-7526

#50A~9199

price code 25

kingwood showcase

#50A~2619

price code 19

oakbrook

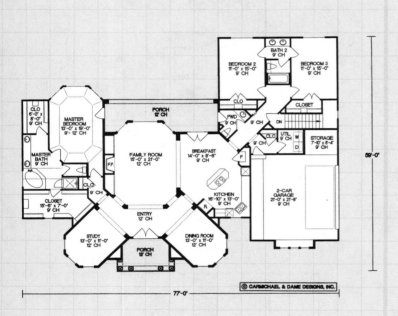

2517 total sq. ft.

Pleasing views highlight this uniquely shaped study.

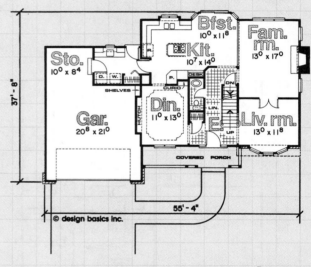

1093	main floor
905	second floor
1998	total sq. ft.

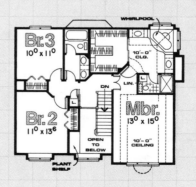

An extended area in the back of this garage offers plenty of room for a work bench and tool cabinets.

a study of home ~ special places

#50A~24029

price code 15

feldon

This home's front porch was meant to be used with its six-foot depth, nine-foot ceiling and lovely columns.

© W. L. Martin Designs

1539 total sq. ft.

NOTE: 9 ft. main level walls

ORIGINAL DRAFT
C
ALL PLANS HAVE BEEN REGISTERED WITH THE U.S. COPYRIGHT OFFICE

#50A~2649

price code 26

hillcrest

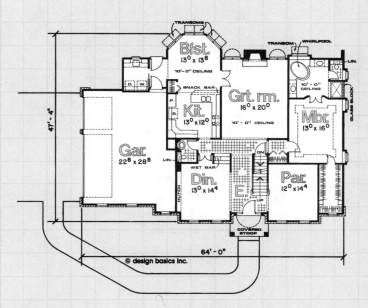

© design basics inc.

The parlor in the front of this home could also be used for an office.

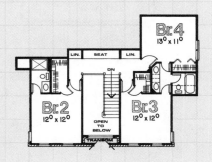

1865 main floor
774 second floor
2639 total sq. ft.

design basics inc.
HOME PLAN DESIGN SERVICE   800-947-7526

#50A~24043
price code 16

inverness

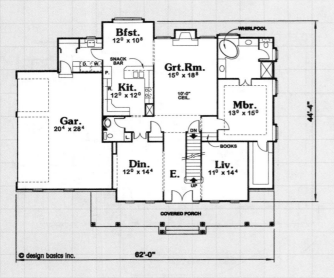

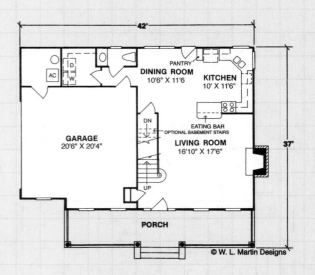

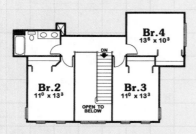

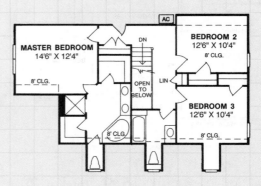

1755 main floor
693 second floor
2448 total sq. ft.

NOTE: 9 ft. main level walls

the living room in the front of this home could also be used as a home office or media room.

731 main floor
901 second floor
1632 total sq. ft.

NOTE: 9 ft. main level walls

the master suite features two walk-in closets and another roomy closet just outside the bedroom.

a study of home ~ special places

kirby farm

#50A-9174
price code 26

stanton showcase

Much of this attic enjoys a ten-foot ceiling, providing added versatility.

1844   main floor
794   second floor
2638   total sq. ft.

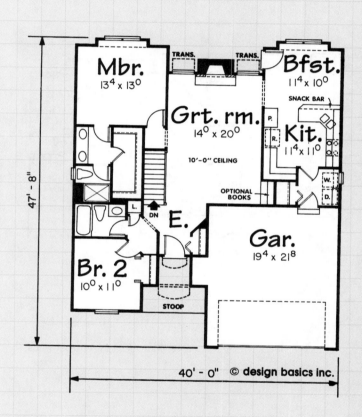

1212   total sq. ft.

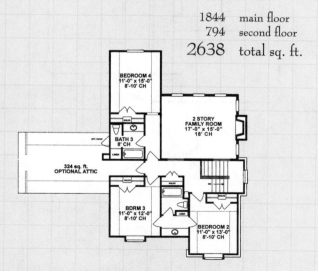

Unfinished Attic Space Adds 324 Sq. Ft.

A built-in bookcase in the great room could also be converted to a computer area or a wet bar.

#50A-2326
price code 21

greensboro

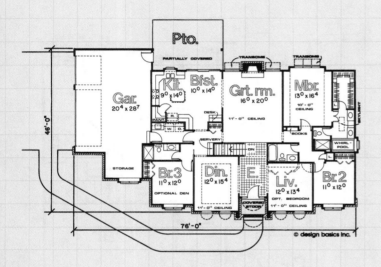

2172 total sq. ft.

NOTE: 9 ft. main level walls

A generous window in the garage makes the extended area an ideal spot for a work area.

#50A-24044
price code 18

farrelton

© W. L. Martin Designs

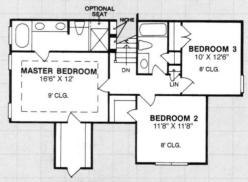

1014 main floor
809 second floor
1823 total sq. ft.

the dining room in the front of the home could also be used as a study or home office.

a study of home ~ special places

#50A~24045

price code 12

glenco

#50A~3381

price code 20

amanda

Front and rear porches offer additional living space outdoors.

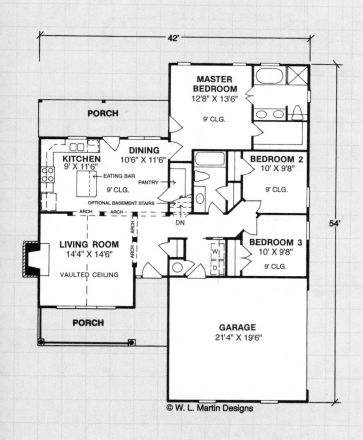

42'

PORCH

MASTER BEDROOM
12'8" X 13'6"
9' CLG.

KITCHEN
9' X 11'6"

DINING
10'6" X 11'6"
9' CLG.

EATING BAR

PANTRY

BEDROOM 2
10' X 9'8"
9' CLG.

OPTIONAL BASEMENT STAIRS

ARCH   ARCH

DN

ARCH   ARCH

LIVING ROOM
14'4" X 14'6"

VAULTED CEILING

BEDROOM 3
10' X 9'8"
9' CLG.

W | D

54'

PORCH

GARAGE
21'4" X 19'6"

© W. L. Martin Designs

1263 total sq. ft.

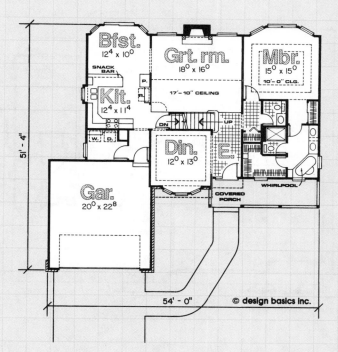

Bfst.
12⁴ x 10⁰

SNACK BAR

Grt. rm.
18⁰ x 16⁰

17'- 10" CEILING

Mbr.
15⁰ x 15⁰
10'- 0" CLG.

Kit.
12⁴ x 11⁴

P.

DN

UP

Din.
12⁰ x 13⁰

W. | D.

Gar.
20⁰ x 22⁸

COVERED PORCH

WHIRLPOOL

5'- 4"

54' - 0"

© design basics inc.

1426 main floor
611 second floor
2037 total sq. ft.

Br. 3
12⁴ x 10¹⁰

OPEN TO BELOW

DN

Br. 4
12⁴ x 10⁰

Br. 2
12⁰ x 11⁴

PLANT SHELF

In smaller families, the fourth bedroom could be used as a home office, exercise room or hobby room.

#50A~2285
price code 21

prairie

#50A~24051
price code 15

cabrie

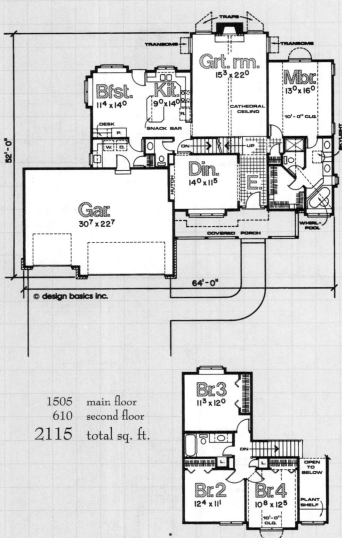

Grt. rm.
15³ x 22⁰

Bfst.
11⁴ x 14⁰

Kit.
9⁰ x 14⁰

Mbr.
13⁰ x 16⁰

CATHEDRAL CEILING

10'-0" CLG.

DESK

SNACK BAR

DN

UP

Din.
14⁰ x 11⁵

Gar.
30⁷ x 22⁷

COVERED PORCH

WHIRL-POOL

SKYLIGHT

TRANSOM   TRANSOM

TRAPS

52'-0"

64'-0"

© design basics inc.

Br. 3
11³ x 12⁰

DN

OPEN TO BELOW

Br. 2
12⁴ x 11¹¹

Br. 4
10⁸ x 12⁵

10'-0" CLG.

PLANT SHELF

1505   main floor
610   second floor
2115   total sq. ft.

This sunny breakfast area with two boxed windows also features a built-in desk — perfect for a computer station.

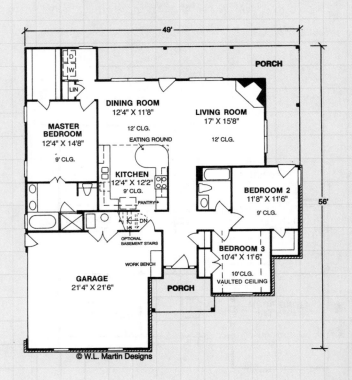

PORCH

DINING ROOM
12'4" X 11'8"
12' CLG.

LIVING ROOM
17' X 15'8"
12' CLG.

MASTER BEDROOM
12'4" X 14'8"
9' CLG.

EATING ROUND

KITCHEN
12'4" X 12'2"
9' CLG.

PANTRY

BEDROOM 2
11'8" X 11'6"
9' CLG.

DN

OPTIONAL BASEMENT STAIRS

GARAGE
21'4" X 21'6"

WORK BENCH

BEDROOM 3
10'4" X 11'6"
10' CLG.
VAULTED CEILING

PORCH

D
W
LIN

49'

56'

© W.L. Martin Designs

1541   total sq. ft.

A large wrapping porch is accessed from the dining room and bedroom #2.

a study of home ~ special places

#50A~9189
price code 22 alexander court

the workshop in this garage enjoys natural sunlight.

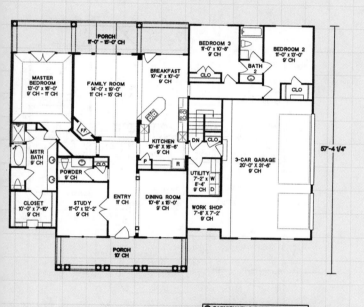

© CARMICHAEL & DAME DESIGNS, INC.

67'-8"

57'-4 1/4"

2256 total sq. ft.

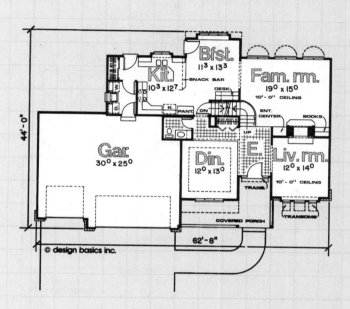

© design basics inc.

44'-0"

62'-8"

1268 main floor
1075 second floor
2343 total sq. ft.

A centrally located desk in the breakfast area makes a handy spot for a computer.

#50A-8095
price code 16

sun valley

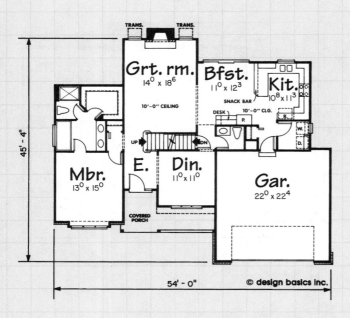

Grt. rm.
14⁰ x 18⁶
10'-0" CEILING

Bfst.
11⁰ x 12³

Kit.
10⁸ x 11³

SNACK BAR

DESK 10'-0" CLG.

Mbr.
13⁰ x 15⁰

E.

Din.
11⁰ x 11⁰

UP

DN

Gar.
22⁰ x 22⁴

COVERED PORCH

45' - 4"

54' - 0"

© design basics inc.

1298   main floor
396   second floor
1694   total sq. ft.

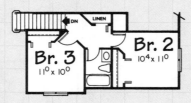

DN   LINEN

Br. 3
11⁰ x 10⁰

Br. 2
10⁴ x 11⁰

With a pantry next door for software, extra controllers and supplies, the desk in this breakfast area is an ideal spot for a computer.

#50A-3577
price code 17

bennett

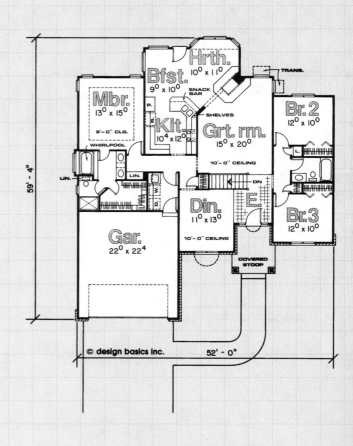

Mbr.
13⁰ x 15⁰
9'-0" CLG.

WHIRLPOOL

LIN.

Bfst.
9⁰ x 10⁰

Hrth.
10⁰ x 11⁰

SNACK BAR

Kit.
10⁴ x 12⁰

SHELVES

Grt. rm.
15⁰ x 20⁰
10'-0" CEILING

Br. 2
12⁰ x 10⁰

Br. 3
12⁰ x 10⁰

Din.
11⁰ x 13⁰
10'-0" CEILING

E.

DN

Gar.
22⁰ x 22⁴

COVERED STOOP

TRANS.

59' - 4"

© design basics inc.   52' - 0"

1782   total sq. ft.

A lovely hearth room features bayed windows and shares a three-sided fireplace.

a study of home ~ special places

#50A~5503

price code 25

briarton

A loveseat and chair fit perfectly in the master bedroom's bayed sitting area.

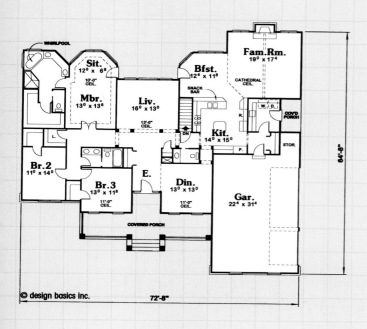

Sit.
12⁰ x 6⁸
10'-0" CEIL.

Mbr.
13⁰ x 13⁶

Liv.
16⁰ x 13⁰
13'-0" CEIL.

Bfst.
12⁴ x 11⁸

Fam.Rm.
19⁰ x 17⁴
CATHEDRAL CEIL.

SNACK BAR

WHIRLPOOL

Br. 2
11⁰ x 14⁰

Br. 3
13⁰ x 11⁸
11'-0" CEIL.

Kit.
14⁰ x 15⁰

Din.
13⁰ x 13⁰
11'-0" CEIL.

Gar.
22⁴ x 31⁴

W. D.

COV'D PORCH

STOR.

E.

DN

COVERED PORCH

© design basics inc.   72'-8"

64'-8"

2586 total sq. ft.

NOTE: 9 ft. main level walls

#50A~2723

price code 26

armburst

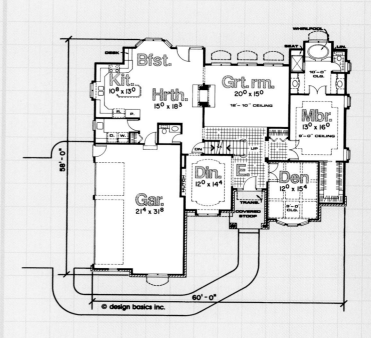

DESK

Bfst.

Kit.
10⁸ x 13⁰

Hrth.
15⁰ x 18³

Grt. rm.
20⁰ x 15⁰
12'-10" CEILING

WHIRLPOOL
SEAT
10'-0" CLG.

Mbr.
13⁰ x 16⁰
9'-0" CEILING

D. W.

Gar.
21⁴ x 31⁸

Din.
12⁰ x 14⁴

E.

Den
12⁰ x 15⁴
9'-0" CLG.

DN

UP

HUTCH

TRANSL.

COVERED STOOP

58'-0"

60'-0"

© design basics inc.

1972   main floor
673   second floor
2645   total sq. ft.

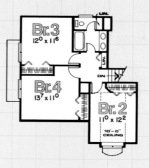

WHIRLPOOL

Br.3
12⁰ x 11⁶

Br.4
13⁷ x 11⁰

Br. 2
11⁰ x 12²
10'-0" CEILING

LIN.

LIN.

DN

Special details in this stylish den include a spider-beamed ceiling, bayed windows and French doors.

hearth rooms

As society has grown more casual, families and friends have gravitated toward the back of the home - and the kitchen. Cozy hearth rooms just off the kitchen have become increasingly popular. these intimate areas provide the perfect spot to enjoy a cup of coffee and read the morning paper, entertain a few friends after dinner, gather the family to catch up on one another's day or play cards together.

#50A-2458
price code 29

the hartford

2084   main floor
848   second floor
2932   total sq. ft.

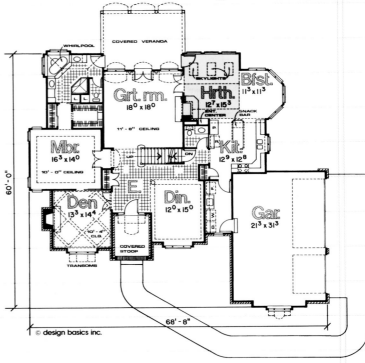

© design basics inc.

This hearth room is shown for example purposes only and is not from the hartford.

Imagine cozy evenings in the hartford's hearth room — gazing at glowing embers in the see-thru fireplace.

Photo By: Phil Bell

www.designbasics.com

the kingsbury

#50A~2445 price code 28

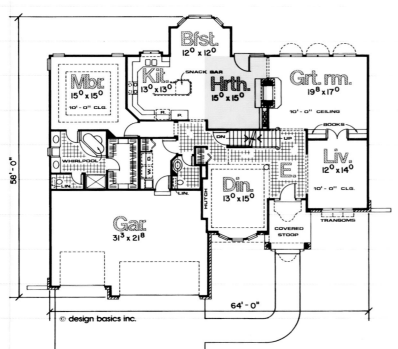

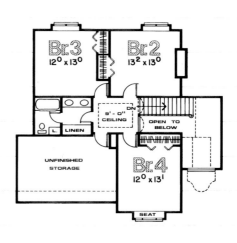

2073 main floor
741 second floor
2814 total sq. ft.

Unfinished Storage adds 261 Sq. Ft.

this open hearth room provides a charming spot for guests to mingle between the great room and the kitchen

the santa fe

#50A~6803   price code 19

Bayed windows in this hearth room provide a pleasing view to an open courtyard.

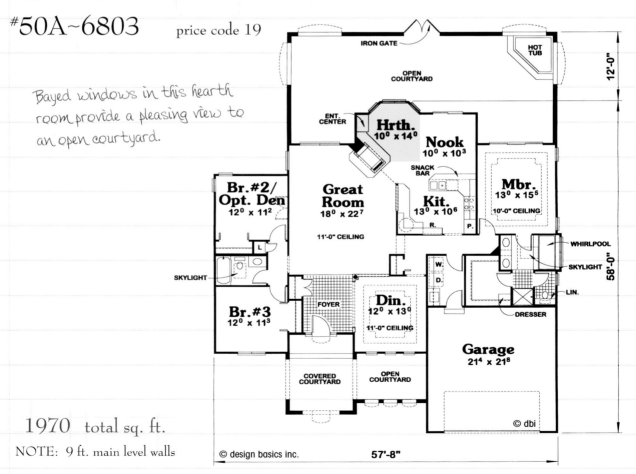

1970 total sq. ft.

NOTE: 9 ft. main level walls

the kincaid

#50A~6710   price code 12

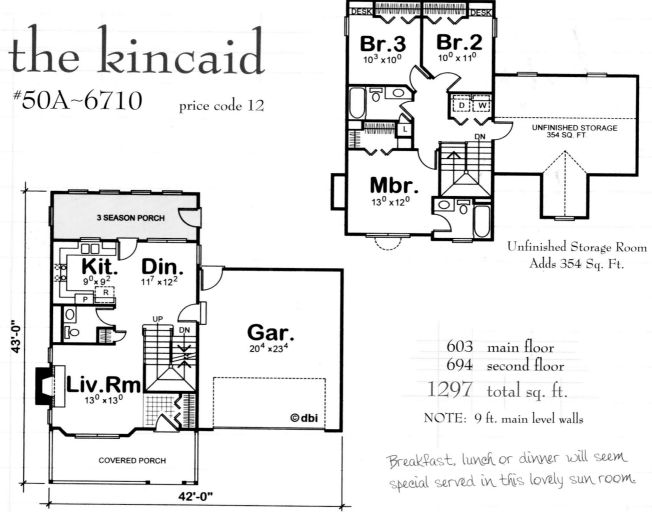

3 SEASON PORCH

Kit.
$9^0 \times 9^2$

Din.
$11^7 \times 12^2$

P   R

UP   DN

Gar.
$20^4 \times 23^4$

Liv.Rm
$13^0 \times 13^0$

©dbi

COVERED PORCH

43'-0"

42'-0"

DESK   DESK

Br.3
$10^3 \times 10^0$

Br.2
$10^0 \times 11^0$

D   W

L

DN

Mbr.
$13^0 \times 12^0$

UNFINISHED STORAGE
354 SQ. FT.

Unfinished Storage Room
Adds 354 Sq. Ft.

603   main floor
694   second floor
1297   total sq. ft.

NOTE: 9 ft. main level walls

Breakfast, lunch or dinner will seem special served in this lovely sun room.

design basics inc.
HOME PLAN DESIGN SERVICE

the creswell

#50A~5458   price code 18

French doors lead to a lovely sun room with sloped ceiling.

Garden Room Adds 124 Sq. Ft.

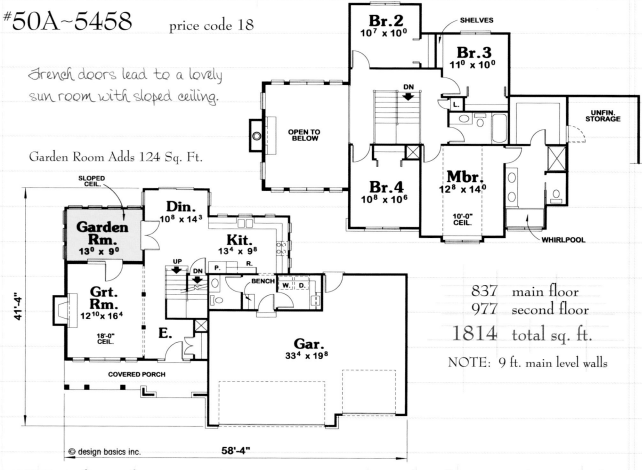

837   main floor
977   second floor
1814   total sq. ft.

NOTE: 9 ft. main level walls

© design basics inc.

the alliston

#50A~5497   price code 23

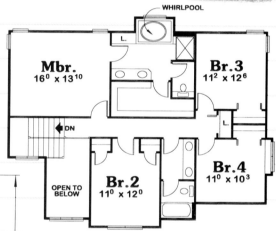

WHIRLPOOL

Mbr.
16⁰ x 13¹⁰

Br.3
11² x 12⁶

L.

DN

Br.2
11⁰ x 12⁰

Br.4
11⁰ x 10³

OPEN TO BELOW

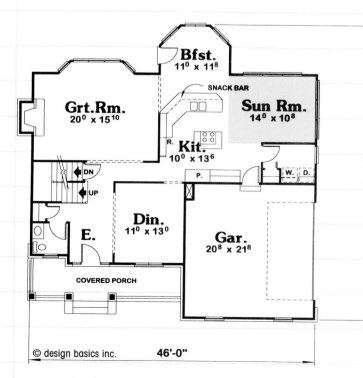

Bfst.
11⁰ x 11⁸

Grt.Rm.
20⁰ x 15¹⁰

SNACK BAR

Sun Rm.
14⁰ x 10⁸

R. **Kit.**
10⁰ x 13⁶

DN
UP

P.

W. D.

Din.
11⁰ x 13⁰

E.

Gar.
20⁸ x 21⁸

COVERED PORCH

48'-0"

46'-0"

© design basics inc.

1256   main floor
1108   second floor
2364   total sq. ft.

NOTE: 9 ft. main level walls

this open sun room floods the kitchen with natural light.

design basics inc
HOME PLAN DESIGN SERVICE

800-947-7526

65

the hopewell

#50A~6705   price code 16

a sun room off the great room provides extra space when entertaining.

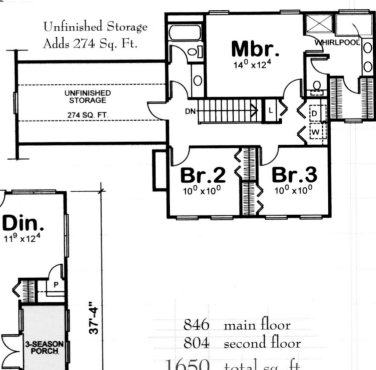

Unfinished Storage
Adds 274 Sq. Ft.

Mbr.
14⁰ x 12⁴

WHIRLPOOL

UNFINISHED STORAGE
274 SQ. FT.

DN   L

D

W

Br. 2
10⁰ x 10⁰

Br. 3
10⁰ x 10⁰

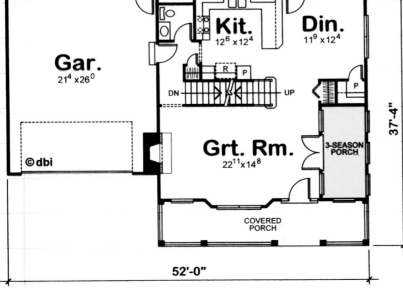

Gar.
21⁴ x 26⁰

© dbi

Kit.
12⁶ x 12⁴

Din.
11⁹ x 12⁴

DN   UP   P

Grt. Rm.
22¹¹ x 14⁸

3-SEASON PORCH

37'-4"

COVERED PORCH

52'-0"

846   main floor
804   second floor
1650   total sq. ft.

NOTE: 9 ft. main level walls

sun rooms
cont'd

Here are some tips for designing and decorating a sun room:

• Southern exposures are best for capturing the most daylight, but may be too hot in warm climates. In cool regions, placing a sun room on a true east-west axis will allow it to collect heat throughout most of the day.

• Choose windows with high R-values and low U-values - double pane or triple pane glass.

• Ventilation from workable windows and a ceiling fan are generally welcome features.

• Shades or motorized awnings on ceilings and walls reduce glare and overheating.

• Brick, tile, cement, wood and vinyl are appropriate floor coverings. Quarry tile absorbs heat to stay warmer in the evenings.

dens

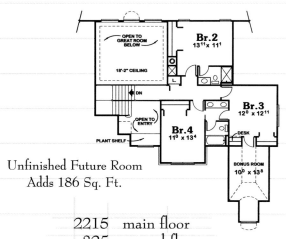

Bfst.
14⁰ x 10⁸

Grt. rm.
18⁰ x 15¹⁰
18'-2" CEILING

Kit.
15⁴ x 16⁰

SNACK BAR

Hrth.
14⁰ x 16⁰

DBL OVEN/ MICRO

PANTRY

Mbr.
15⁰ x 16⁰
11'-0" CEILING

DN
UP
18'-2" CEILING

F. D W.

E.

Din.
11⁰ x 15⁹

Den
12⁰ x 13⁰

COVERED STOOP

Gar.
22⁰ x 32⁰

66'-0"

66'-0"

In times past, dens were generally masculine rooms furnished in dark wood and leather furniture and filled with big, heavy books and the smell of pipe tobacco. While today's dens are still considered adult sanctuaries, they've become rooms men and women are equally at home in. Ideally, a den should be located away from the home's busiest areas and should definitely have a door to close out distractions.

#50A~4144
price code 30

the marlow

OPEN TO GREAT ROOM BELOW

Br. 2
13¹¹ x 11¹

18'-2" CEILING

DN

Br. 3
12⁰ x 12¹¹

OPEN TO ENTRY

Br. 4
11⁰ x 13⁴

PLANT SHELF

DESK

BONUS ROOM
10⁰ x 13⁸

Unfinished Future Room
Adds 186 Sq. Ft.

A cathedral ceiling, a fireplace and French doors add ambiance in the marlow's cozy den.

2215	main floor
825	second floor
3040	**total sq. ft.**

NOTE: 9 ft. main level walls

www.designbasics.com

the kempton court

#50A~9169   price code 30

An octagon-shaped den with tall, arched windows offers a scenic spot to read or reflect.

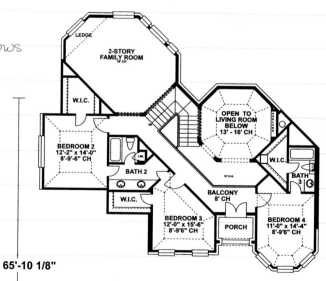

65'-10 1/8"

67'-1"

© CARMICHAEL & DAME DESIGNS, INC.

2112   main floor
982   second floor
3094   total sq. ft.

the windrush estate

#50A~9198   price code 18

French doors lead to a charming study with bayed windows and cathedral ceiling.

1876 total sq. ft.

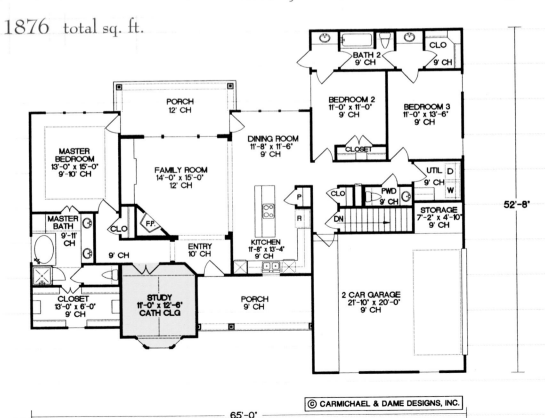

© CARMICHAEL & DAME DESIGNS, INC.

the thornhill

#50A~3494

price code 28

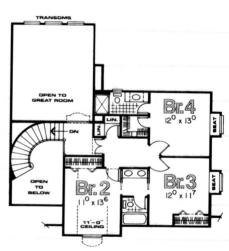

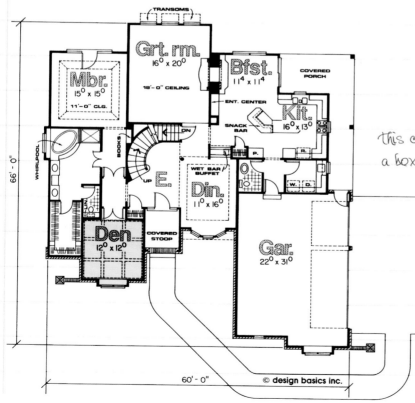

this charming den features french doors, a boxed window and spider-beamed ceiling.

2041   main floor
809   second floor
2850   total sq. ft.

NOTE: 9 ft. main level walls

© design basics inc.

Photo By: Phil Bell

This sitting room is shown for example purposes only and is not from the edgewood

Bfst. 12⁰ x 12⁰

SNACK BAR

Fam. rm. 20⁰ x 16⁰

CATHEDRAL CEILING

Kit. 14⁰ x 12⁰

Din. 14⁰ x 12⁰

58' - 0"

TRANS.

Liv. rm. 13⁰ x 15⁰

11' - 0" CEILING

UP

Gar. 20⁴ x 31⁴

Den 13⁰ x 14⁸

TRANSOMS

COVERED STOOP

60' - 0"

© design basics inc.

#50A~2839

price code 30

the edgewood

Special ceiling detail and bayed windows create a lovely retreat off the edgewood's master bedroom.

www.designbasics.com

sitting rooms

The fast-paced lifestyles most of us lead have made incorporating quiet havens into our homes more important than ever. At the end of the day, we need a refuge to come to, a quiet, secluded place to wind down. Often located off a master bedroom, sitting rooms are delightful spots to have a cup of coffee and read the newspaper, to reflect on things that really matter, to enjoy a private conversation with a spouse or to have one-on-one time with a child.

1631 main floor
1426 second floor
3057 total sq. ft.

NOTE: 9 ft. main level walls

16'-0" CEILING

Mbr. 16⁰ x 22⁰

DRESSER

WHIRLPOOL

Br. 3 13⁰ x 12⁰

DN   LIN.

Br. 4 11⁰ x 14⁰

OPEN TO BELOW

Br. 2 13⁰ x 12⁰

TRANSOM

SEAT

the fairchild

#50A~2733   price code 39

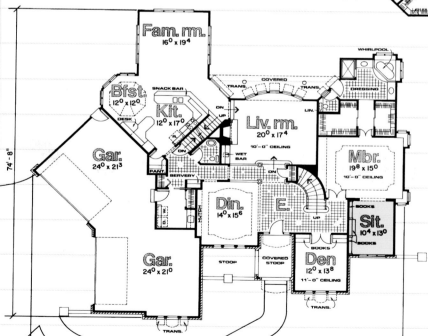

Br. 2
13⁰ x 17⁴
10'-0" CLG.

Br. 4
12⁰ x 15⁶
10'-0" CEILING

SEAT

LINEN

BOOKS

DN

Br. 3
14⁰ x 15⁶

OPEN TO BELOW

DN

TRANSOMS

Fam. rm.
16⁰ x 19⁴

Bfst.
12⁰ x 12⁰

Kit.
12⁰ x 17⁰

SNACK BAR

DESK

COVERED

TRANS.

TRANS.

WHIRLPOOL

DRESSING

LIN.

Liv. rm.
20⁰ x 17⁴

10'-0" CEILING

DN   UP

Gar.
24⁰ x 21³

WET BAR

PANT

SERVERY

Mbr.
19⁸ x 15⁰

10'-0" CEILING

DN

Din.
14⁰ x 15⁶

E.

UP

BOOKS

Sit.
10⁴ x 13⁰

BOOKS

Gar.
24⁰ x 21⁰

STOOP

COVERED STOOP

Den
12⁰ x 13⁸

11'-0" CEILING

BOOKS

TRANS.

TRANS.

74'-8"

85'-5"

© design basics inc.

this sitting room off the master bedroom is the perfect spot to read a great book - from a wall lined with bookshelves.

2813	main floor
1091	second floor
3904	**total sq. ft.**

NOTE: 9 ft. main level walls

design basics inc.
HOME PLAN DESIGN SERVICE   800-947-7526

the gainsborough

#50A~2043   price code 32

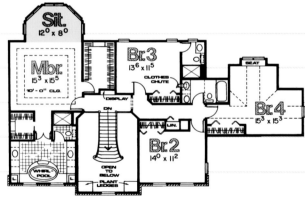

1717	main floor
1518	second floor
3235	total sq. ft.

NOTE: 9 ft. main level walls

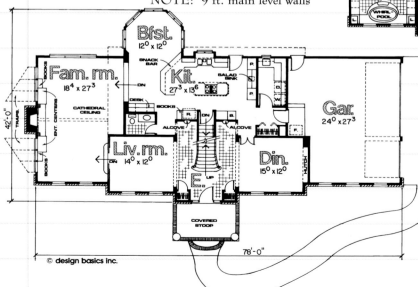

What could be more relaxing than enjoying a good cup of coffee and the Sunday paper in this bayed sitting/reading area?

a study of home ~ special places

the philipsburg

#50A~5520

price code 26

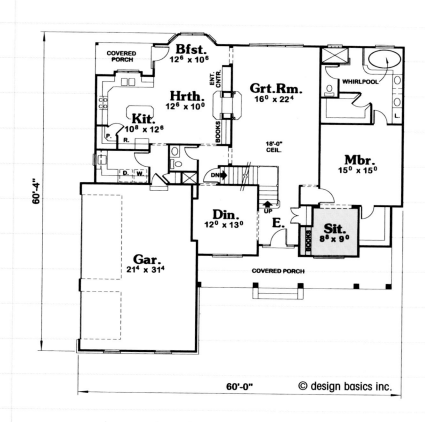

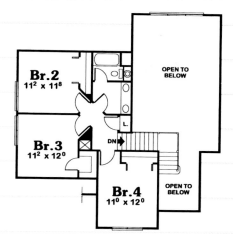

Br.2
11² x 11⁸

Br.3
11² x 12⁰

Br.4
11⁰ x 12⁰

OPEN TO BELOW

OPEN TO BELOW

DN

L

COVERED PORCH

Bfst.
12⁶ x 10⁶

Hrth.
12⁶ x 10⁰

ENT. CNTR.

Grt.Rm.
16⁰ x 22⁴

WHIRLPOOL

Kit.
10⁸ x 12⁶

P.   R.

BOOKS

18'-0" CEIL.

Mbr.
15⁰ x 15⁰

D   W

DN

Din.
12⁰ x 13⁰

E.

UP

Sit.
8⁸ x 9⁰

BOOKS

60'-4"

Gar.
21⁴ x 31⁴

COVERED PORCH

60'-0"

© design basics inc.

1955   main floor
660   second floor
2615   total sq. ft.

NOTE: 9 ft. main level walls

this cozy sitting area enjoys a view
of the porch and a built-in bookcase.

800-947-7526

special places to
Use However you Choose

F.R.O.G. (finished room over garage)

One of the hottest new trends in home design is the incorporation of Finished Rooms Over Garages. F.R.O.G.s are generally deep rooms which run the full length of the garage. Their naturally sloping ceilings provide a charming atmosphere similar to a finished attic. Because of their separation from the rest of the house, they work well as an apartment for an older child; an artist's studio; a home office or a hobby, exercise or play room. Here are some practical points to remember in planning a F.R.O.G.:

• If the area will be used as a media room, choose a solid door and add extra insulation in walls, ceiling and floor to contain loud music or video game sound effects. If more sound absorption is needed, walls can be covered with polyester batting and fabric.

• To make the ceiling seem higher, unite walls and ceiling in a single, light color. When choosing a paint color, remember colors appear stronger in larger areas. To counter this, choose a lighter value of the same hue.

• Because F.R.O.G.s are usually longer than they are wide, create an illusion of width by grouping furnishings on an angle. Locate chairs, sofas, beds and desks close to the eaves where the ceiling is too low to walk or stand under. Decorator panels can divide the space for different functions.

www.designbasics.com

the atwell

#50A~7217

price code 19

this roomy area over the garage would make a delightful play room or hobby area.

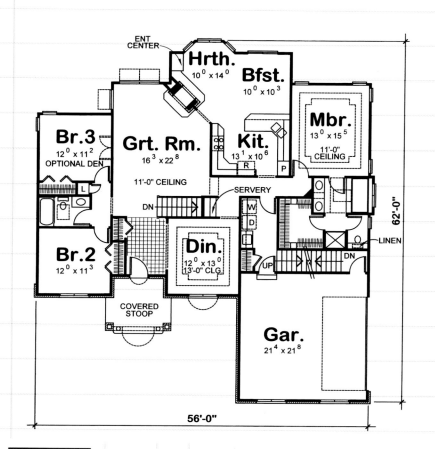

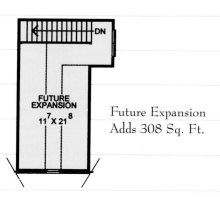

Future Expansion
Adds 308 Sq. Ft.

1995 total sq. ft.

NOTE: 9 ft. main level walls

the lena

#50A~24099   price code 20

2040 total sq. ft.

ATTIC

FUTURE GAMEROOM
18'4" X 24'6"
8' CLG.
ADDS 409 SQ. FT.

DN

SLOPE 5' TO 8'

Future Game Room Adds 409 Sq. Ft.

the game room could easily be divided into two areas for multiple uses.

60'

BEDROOM 2
11'4" X 11'
9' CLG.

NOOK
10' X 11'4"
9' CLG.

PORCH

SLOPE 9' TO 11'

MASTER BEDROOM
13'4" X 16'
11' CLG.

DESK

PANTRY

EATING BAR

BEDROOM 3
12' X 13'
9' CLG.

KITCHEN
12'4" X 12'

ISLAND

DW

LIVING ROOM
16' X 20'
11' CLG.
SLOPE 9' TO 11'

11'CLG.

LIN

OPTIONAL BASEMENT STAIRS

LAUND.

UP

DN

ARCH

ARCH

FOYER
10' CLG.

D W

WORKBENCH

GARAGE
21'4" X 24'6"

DINING
11'8" X 15'8"
10' CLG.

56'

PORCH

a study of home ~ special places

the piermont

#50A~7216   price code 26

this home boasts a spacious G.R.D.G. and a lovely loft with a built-in window seat.

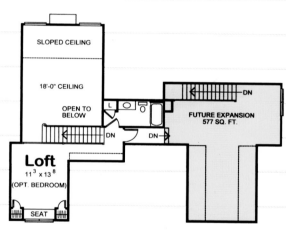

SLOPED CEILING

18'-0" CEILING

OPEN TO BELOW

FUTURE EXPANSION 577 SQ. FT.

Loft
11³ x 13⁸
(OPT. BEDROOM)

SEAT

Future Expansion Adds 577 Sq. Ft.

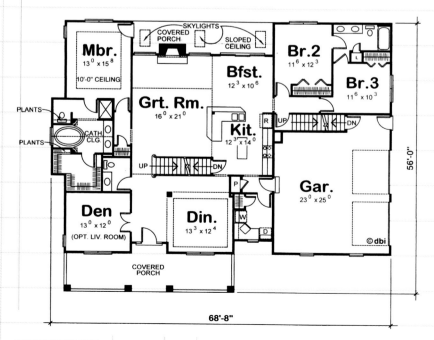

Mbr.
13⁰ x 15⁸
10'-0" CEILING

SKYLIGHTS
COVERED PORCH
SLOPED CEILING

Bfst.
12³ x 10⁶

Br.2
11⁶ x 12³

Grt. Rm.
16⁰ x 21⁰

Br.3
11⁶ x 10³

PLANTS

CATH CLG.

Kit.
12³ x 14⁰

Den
13⁰ x 12⁰
(OPT. LIV. ROOM)

Din.
13³ x 12⁴

Gar.
23⁰ x 25⁰

©dbi

COVERED PORCH

56'-0"

68'-8"

2629 total sq. ft.

NOTE: 9 ft. main level walls

HOME PLAN DESIGN SERVICE   800-947-7526

79

the kenton

#50A~6734   price code 14

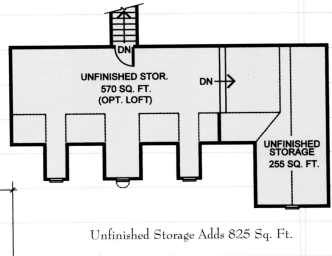

UNFINISHED STOR.
570 SQ. FT.
(OPT. LOFT)

DN →

DN

UNFINISHED
STORAGE
255 SQ. FT.

Unfinished Storage Adds 825 Sq. Ft.

1495 total sq. ft.

NOTE: 9 ft. main level walls

this spacious J.R.O.G. offers countless options. Part of it could even be used as a loft with a few modifications.

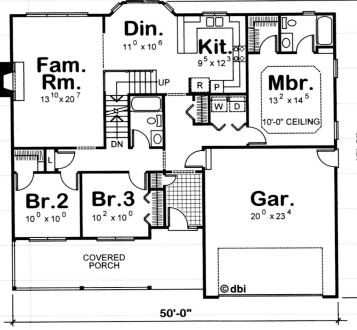

Din.
11⁰ x 10⁶

Kit.
9⁵ x 12³

Fam. Rm.
13¹⁰ x 20⁷

UP

R P

Mbr.
13² x 14⁵
10'-0" CEILING

W D

DN

Br.2
10⁰ x 10⁰

Br.3
10² x 10⁰

Gar.
20⁰ x 23⁴

COVERED PORCH

©dbi

47'-0"

50'-0"

a study of home ~ special places

the greenleaf

#50A~24101   price code 26

With ample windows and an eight to ten-foot sloped ceiling, this game room would be the perfect spot for a pool table.

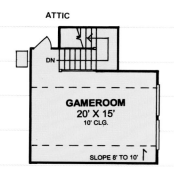

ATTIC

DN

GAMEROOM
20' X 15'
10' CLG.

SLOPE 8' TO 10'

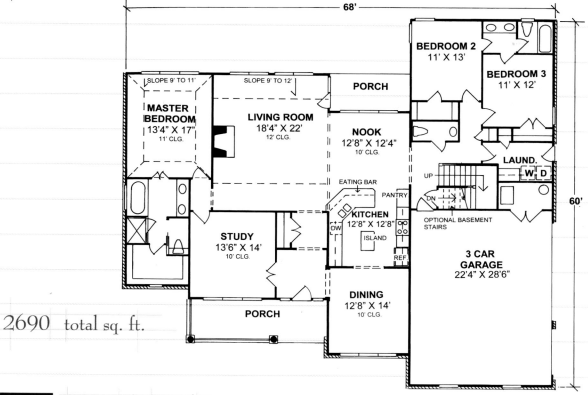

68'

60'

BEDROOM 2
11' X 13'

BEDROOM 3
11' X 12'

SLOPE 9' TO 11'

SLOPE 9' TO 12'

PORCH

MASTER BEDROOM
13'4" X 17"
11' CLG.

LIVING ROOM
18'4" X 22'
12' CLG.

NOOK
12'8" X 12'4"
10' CLG.

LAUND.

W D

EATING BAR

PANTRY

UP

STUDY
13'6" X 14'
10' CLG.

DW

KITCHEN
12'8" X 12'8"

ISLAND

REF.

DN

OPTIONAL BASEMENT STAIRS

3 CAR GARAGE
22'4" X 28'6"

DINING
12'8" X 14'
10' CLG.

PORCH

2690 total sq. ft.

the coventry

#50A~6735   price code 15

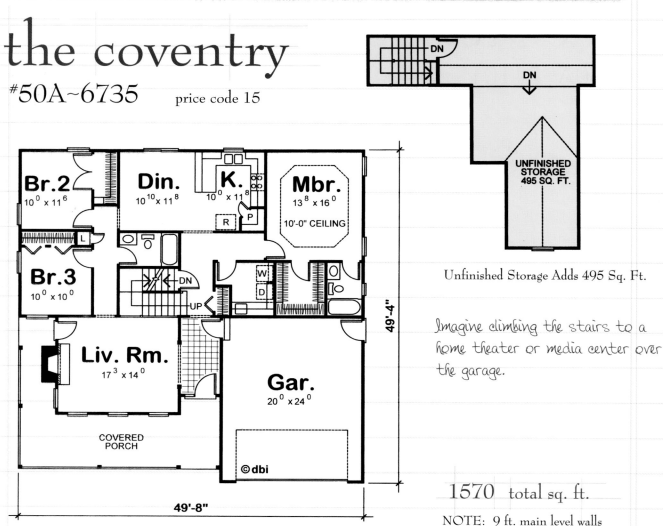

Br.2 10⁰ x 11⁶

Din. 10¹⁰ x 11⁸

K. 10⁰ x 11⁸

Mbr. 13⁸ x 16⁰   10'-0" CEILING

R   P

Br.3 10⁰ x 10⁰

DN   UP

W   D

Liv. Rm. 17³ x 14⁰

Gar. 20⁰ x 24⁰

COVERED PORCH

©dbi

49'-4"

49'-8"

DN

DN

UNFINISHED STORAGE 495 SQ. FT.

Unfinished Storage Adds 495 Sq. Ft.

Imagine climbing the stairs to a home theater or media center over the garage.

1570 total sq. ft.

NOTE: 9 ft. main level walls

lofts

Great rooms with soaring ceilings have made lofts a popular addition to many new homes. With their open, airy space, dramatic views and semi-private seclusion, lofts offer interesting architecture and unique ambiance. Highly adaptable, they can be used as home offices, computer areas, guest bedrooms, play areas, game rooms or cozy reading spots.

Main floor plan

- BUILT-IN DRESSER
- CATHEDRAL CEILING
- **Bfst.** 11⁰ x 10⁰
- **Grt.Rm.** 16⁸ x 18⁰
- UP
- SNACK BAR
- **Kit.** 15¹¹ x 14³
- WHIRLPOOL TUB
- 54'-0"
- DN
- P.
- W. / D.
- L.
- **E.**
- **Mbr.** 16⁰ x 14⁰
- COVERED STOOP
- **Gar.** 22⁰ x 22⁴
- 51'-4"
- © design basics inc.

1640   main floor
711   second floor
2351   total sq. ft.

NOTE: 9 ft. main level walls

Second floor plan

- CATHEDRAL CEILING
- OPEN TO BELOW
- **Br.2** 13⁸ x 11⁰
- DN
- L.
- **Br.3** 11⁰ x 12⁴
- **Loft** 12⁰ x 15⁴
- BOOKS
- BOOKS
- OPTIONAL BEDROOM

#50A~4082
price code 23

the kenneth

The kenneth's spacious loft provides a stunning view into the dramatic great room, a boxed window and built-in bookcases.

design basics inc.
HOME PLAN DESIGN SERVICE

800-947-7526

the troon manor

#50A~9166   price code 23

Studying will be more pleasant in this beautiful, airy study loft.

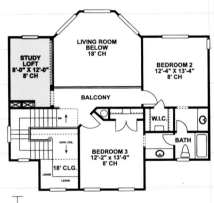

1649   main floor
712   second floor
2361   total sq. ft.

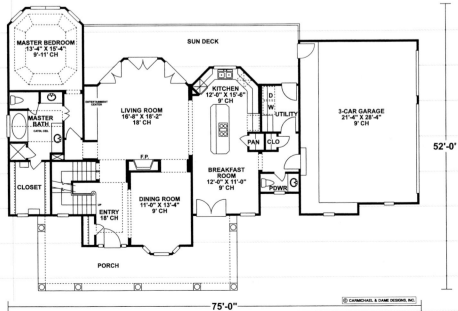

the claiborne

#50A~24034 price code 18

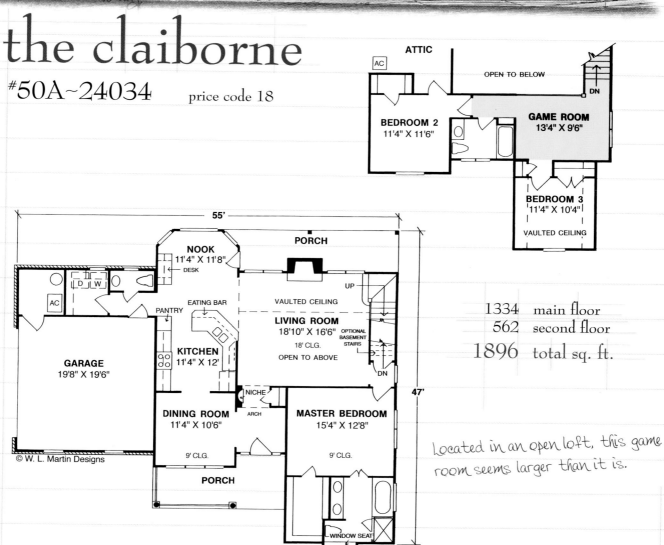

ATTIC

AC

OPEN TO BELOW

DN

BEDROOM 2
11'4" X 11'6"

GAME ROOM
13'4" X 9'6"

BEDROOM 3
11'4" X 10'4"

VAULTED CEILING

55'

NOOK
11'4" X 11'8"

← DESK

PORCH

D W

AC

PANTRY

EATING BAR

VAULTED CEILING

UP

KITCHEN
11'4" X 12'

LIVING ROOM
18'10" X 16'6"

18' CLG.

OPEN TO ABOVE

OPTIONAL BASEMENT STAIRS

DN

GARAGE
19'8" X 19'6"

NICHE

ARCH

DINING ROOM
11'4" X 10'6"

MASTER BEDROOM
15'4" X 12'8"

9' CLG.

9' CLG.

47'

© W. L. Martin Designs

PORCH

WINDOW SEAT

1334 main floor
562 second floor
1896 total sq. ft.

Located in an open loft, this game room seems larger than it is.

DESIGN BASICS' HOME PLAN LIBRARY

1.

2.

18.

17.

16.

15.

1) Impressions of Home™
Homes Designed with the
Look You Want – 100 designs
from 1339' to 4139'. $4.95

2) Impressions of Home™
Homes Designed for the Way
You Live – 100 designs from
1191' to 4228'. $4.95

3) Impressions of Home™ Homes & Places for Real
People – 100 designs from 1341' to 4139'. $4.95

4) Heartland Home Plans™
120 plan ideas designed for everyday practicality.
Warm, unpretentious elevations easily adapt to
individual lifestyles. From 1212' to 2631'. $8.95

5) Reflections of an American Home™ Vol. III
50 photographed home plans with warm remem-
brances of home and beautiful interior presentations.
From 1341' to 3775'. $4.95

6) Photographed Portraits of an American Home™
100 of our finest designs, beautifully photographed
and tastefully presented among charming photo album
memories of "home". A must for any sales center's
coffee table. $14.95

7) Gold Seal™ Home Plan Book Set – 442 of today's
most sought-after one-story, 1 1/2 story and 2-story home
plan ideas. All 5 books for $50.00 or $10.00 each

- Homes of Distinction – 86 plans under 1800'
- Homes of Sophistication – 106 plans, 1800'-2199'
- Homes of Elegance – 107 plans, 2200'-2599'
- Homes of Prominence – 75 plans, 2600'-2999'
- Homes of Grandeur – 68 plans, 3000'-4000'

8) Timeless Legacy™, A Collection of Fine Home
Designs by Carmichael & Dame – 52 breathtaking
luxury home designs from 3300' to 4500'. Includes
artful rear views of each home. $15.00

9) The Homes of Carmichael & Dame™ Vol. II
60 elegant designs from simple to sublime.
From 1751' to 4228'. $9.95

10) *Seasons of Life™
Designs for Reaping the Rewards of Autumn
100 home plans specially tailored to today's
empty-nester. From 1212' to 3904'. $4.95

11) *Seasons of Life™
Designs for Living Summer's Journey – 100 designs
for the move-up buyer. From 1605' to 3775'. $4.95

12) *Seasons of Life™
Designs for Spring's New Beginnings – 100 home
plans for first-time buyers. Presentations unique to
this lifestyle. From 1125' to 2537'. $4.95

13) W.L. Martin Home Designs™
53 beautiful home plans offering outstanding livability.
From 1262' to 3914'. $9.95

14) The Narrow Home Plan™ Collection
258 one-story, 1 1/2 story and 2-story home plans that are
from 26 to 50 feet wide. Many can be joined together to
create customized duplex plans. $14.95

15) Nostalgia Home Plans Collection™
A New Approach to Time-Honored Design
70 designs showcasing enchanting details and unique
"special places." From 1339' to 3480'. $9.95

16) Nostalgia Home Plans Collection™ Vol. II
A New Approach to Time-Honored Design
70 designs bringing back the essence of homes
of the past. $9.95

17) Gold Seal Favorites™ – 100 best selling plans
from the famous Gold Seal™ Collection, including
25 duplex designs. $6.95

18) Easy Living One-Story Designs™
155 one-story home designs from the Gold Seal™,
Heartland Home Plans™ and Timeless Legacy™
collections, together in one plan book. $7.95

*Order the complete Seasons of Life™ set
(all three books) for only $9.00

(800) 947~7526
www.designbasics.com

14.

13.

12.

11.

7.

8.

9.

10.

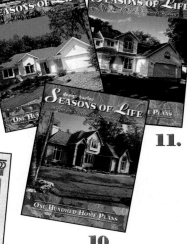

50A

What's in a Design Basics Plan?

1. **Cover Page.** Each Design Basics home plan features the rendered elevation and informative reference sections including: general notes and design criteria;* abbreviations; and symbols for your Design Basics' plan.

2. **Elevations.** Drafted at ¼" scale for the front and ⅛" scale for the rear and sides. All elevations are detailed and an aerial view of the roof is provided, showing all framing members.

3. **Foundations.** Drafted at ¼" scale. Block foundations and basements are standard. We also show the HVAC equipment, structural information,* steel beam and pole locations and the direction and spacing of the floor system above.

4. **Main Level Floor Plan.** ¼" scale. Fully dimensioned from stud to stud for ease of framing. 2"x4" walls are standard. The detailed drawings include such things as structural header locations, framing layout and kitchen layout.

5. **Second Level Floor Plan.** ¼" scale. Dimensioned from stud to stud and drafted to the same degree of detail as the main level floor plan.*

6. **Interior Elevations.** Useful for the cabinet and bidding process, this page shows all kitchen and bathroom cabinets as well as any other cabinet elevations.

7. **Electrical and Sections.** Illustrated on a separate page for clarity, the electrical plan shows suggested electrical layout for the foundation, main and second level floor plans. Typical wall, cantilever, stair, brick and fireplace sections are provided to further explain construction of these areas.

All plan orders received prior to 2:00 p.m. CT will be processed, inspected and shipped out the same afternoon via 2nd business day air within the continental United States. All other product orders will be sent via UPS ground service. Full Technical Support is available for any plan purchase from Design Basics. Our Tech Support Specialists provide unlimited technical support free of charge and answer questions regard construction methods, framing techniques and more. Please call 800-947-7526 for more information.

CONSTRUCTION LICENSE

When you purchase a Design Basics home plan, you receive a Construction License which gives you cer rights in building the home depicted in that plan, including:

No Re-Use Fee. As the original purchaser of a Design Basics home plan, the Construction Lice permits you to build the plan as many times as you like.

Local Modifications. The Construction License allows you to make modifications to your Design Ba plans. We offer a complete custom change service, or you may have the desired changes done locall a qualified draftsman, designer, architect or engineer.

Running Blueprints. Your plans are sent to you on vellum paper that reproduces well on your blue machine. The Construction License authorizes you or your blueprint facility, at your direction, to mak many copies of the plan from the vellum masters as you need for construction purposes.

* Our plans are drafted to meet average conditions and codes in the state of Nebraska, at the time they are designed. Because and requirements can change and may vary from jurisdiction to jurisdiction, Design Basics Inc. cannot warrant compliance with specific code or regulation. All Design Basics plans can be adapted to your local building codes and requirements. It is the respons of the purchaser and/or builder of each plan to see that the structure is built in strict compliance with all governing municipal (city, county, state and federal).

TO ORDER DIRECT: CALL 800-947-7526
MONDAY – FRIDAY 7:00 a.m. – 6:00 p.m. CST

Name _____

Address _____
(For UPS Delivery – Packages cannot be shipped to a P.O. Box.)

Above Address: ☐ business address ☐ residential address

Company _____

Title _____

City _____ State _____ Zip _____

Phone ( ) _____ FAX ( ) _____

☐ VISA **VISA**   ☐ MasterCard **MasterCard**
We appreciate it when you use VISA or MasterCard.

Credit Card: ☐☐☐☐☐☐☐☐☐☐☐☐☐☐☐☐

☐ Check enclosed ☐ AMEX ☐ Discover

Expiration Date: ☐☐ / ☐☐

Signature _____

✓	HOME PLAN PRODUCTS	PLAN #	QTY.	PRICE	SHIPPING & HANDLING	TOTAL
☐	1 Complete Set of Master Reproducible/Modifiable Vellum Prints					$
☐	Add'l. Sets of Blueprints - $20.00 Carmichael & Dame Plans – $40.00					$
☐	Materials & Estimator's Workbook - $50.00 (If Available)					$
☐	Study Print & Furniture Layout Guide™ - $29.95 Carmichael & Dame Study Prints – $29.95 W.L. Martin Study Prints – $29.95					$
☐	Complete Plan Book Library – $150.00					$

• CALL FOR • Shipping & Handling Charges

BOOK NUMBER	BOOK NAME					
						$
						$

CALL 800-947-7526
ASK FOR DEPT. 50A
OR MAIL ORDER TO: **Design Basics**
11112 John Galt Blvd.
Omaha, NE 68137
fax: (402) 331-5507
www.designbasics.com

• No COD Orders • US Funds Only •
NO REFUNDS OR EXCHANGES, PLEASE

Subtotal $ _____

TX Res. Add 6.25% Tax (on Carmichael & Dame plans)
NE Residents Add 6.5% Sales Tax $ _____

design basics inc
HOME PLAN DESIGN SERVICE PRICES SUBJECT TO CHANGE

Total $ _____

PLAN PRICE SCHEDULE

PLAN CODE	TOTAL SQ. FT.	PRICE
9	900' - 999'	$525
10	1000' - 1099'	$535
11	1100' - 1199'	$545
12	1200' - 1299'	$555
13	1300' - 1399'	$565
14	1400' - 1499'	$575
15	1500' - 1599'	$585
16	1600' - 1699'	$595
17	1700' - 1799'	$605
18	1800' - 1899'	$615
19	1900' - 1999'	$625
20	2000' - 2099'	$635
21	2100' - 2199'	$645
22	2200' - 2299'	$655
23	2300' - 2399'	$665
24	2400' - 2499'	$675
25	2500' - 2599'	$685
26	2600' - 2699'	$695
27	2700' - 2799'	$705
28	2800' - 2899'	$715
29	2900' - 2999'	$725
30	3000' - 3099'	$735
31	3100' - 3199'	$745
32	3200' - 3299'	$755
33	3300' - 3399'	$765
34	3400' - 3499'	$775
35	3500' - 3599'	$785
36	3600' - 3699'	$795
37	3700' - 3799'	$805
38	3800' - 3899'	$815
39	3900' - 3999'	$825
40	4000' - 4099'	$835
41	4100' - 4199'	$845
42	4200' - 4299'	$855
43	4300' - 4399'	$865
44	4400' - 4499'	$875
45	4500' - 4599'	$885

PLEASE CALL US FOR CURRENT PRICES
800-947-7526

PRICES SUBJECT TO CHANGE